INSTRUCTIONS ON BOMBING.
PARTS I & II

ISSUED BY T[

40/W.O./4541   PAR[

BRITISH AND GE. ...N BOMBS

December, 1917.

40/W.O./4483   **PART II.**

TRAINING AND EMPLOYMENT OF BOMBERS.

November, 1917.

FireStep
Editions

www.firesteppublishing.com

FireStep Publishing
Gemini House
136-140 Old Shoreham Road
Brighton
BN3 7BD

www.firesteppublishing.com

First published by the General Staff, War Office 1917.
First published in this format by FireStep Editions,
an imprint of FireStep Publishing, in association with
the National Army Museum, 2013.

www.nam.ac.uk

ISBN 978-1-908487-07-0

Cover design FireStep Publishing
Typeset by FireStep Publishing / Graham Hales, Derby
Printed and bound in Great Britain

Please note: *In producing in facsimile from original historical documents, any
imperfections may be reproduced and the quality may be lower than modern
typesetting or cartographic standards.*

NSTRUCTIONS ON BOMBING.
PART I

ISSUED BY THE GENERAL STAFF

0/W.O./4541

PART I.
BRITISH AND GERMAN BOMBS

December, 1917.

This publication cancels:-
S.S. 126 "The Training and Employment of Bombers"
(Revised Edition, September, 1916).
S.S. 406 "Precautions necessary when Firing Rifle Grenades"
(April, 1916).
A.C.I. 289 and 2221 of 1916.
A.C.I. 214 and 762 of 1917.

CONTENTS.

CHAPTER I.

DESCRIPTION OF BRITISH BOMBS AND INSTRUCTIONS FOR THEIR USE.

	PAGE.
INTRODUCTORY NOTE	4
MILLS PATTERN BOMB—	
(a) No. 5, Mark I (hand)	5
(b) No. 23, Marks I, II, and III (rifle), with cup attachment ...	6
(c) No. 36, Mark I (rifle), with discharger	8
BOMB DISCHARGERS—	
(a) For short rifle	10
(b) For 1914 rifle	11
EGG BOMB—	
No. 34, Mark III (hand)	11
HALE PATTERN RIFLE-BOMB—	
(a) No. 3	11
(b) No. 20, Marks I and II	12
(c) No. 24, Marks I and II	13
(d) No. 35, Mark I	14
NEWTON PATTERN RIFLE-BOMB—	
(a) Locally made pattern	15
(b) No. 22, Mark I	15
SMOKE BOMB—	
(a) P. bomb, No. 26	16
(b) No. 27 (hand or rifle)	17
(c) New design	19
GAS BOMBS—	
No. 28	19
SIGNAL BOMBS—	
(a) No. 31 (rifle), daylight	19
(b) No. 32 (rifle), night	20
(c) New design	20
BOMB CARTRIDGES—	
(a) Ballistite	21
(b) 43 grain, Mark II	21
(c) 35 grain (Hales pattern)	21

CHAPTER II.

DESCRIPTION OF GERMAN BOMBS AND INSTRUCTIONS FOR THEIR USE.

GERMAN POLICY	22
PRECAUTIONS (GENERAL)	23
STICK HAND BOMB (TIME)	23
EGG HAND BOMB (TIME)	25

(B 13278A) Wt w 7900—P3105 100M 1/18 H & S P17/713

Smoke Hand Bomb (Time) 26
Gas Hand Bomb (Time) 27
Automatic-lighting Stick Hand Bomb (Time) 28
Stick Hand Bomb (Percussion) 29
Rifle-Bomb, 1913 30
Rifle-Bomb, 1914 31
Fuze Lighters 33
Stick Bomb and Bomb-Throwers, 1915 and 1916 34
Range Table for 1915 or 1916 Bomb-Thrower 39

PLATES.

BRITISH BOMBS.

Plate.
I Mills pattern No. 5, Mark I (hand) 40
II Cup attachment 41
III Mills pattern, No. 23, Mark III (rifle) 42
IV Mills pattern, No. 36, Mark I (rifle) 43
V Bomb discharger 44
VI Egg Bomb, No. 34, Mark III (hand) 45
VII Hale pattern, No. 20, Mark II (rifle) 46
VIII Hale pattern, No. 24, Mark I (rifle) 47
IX Hale pattern, No. 24, Mark II (rifle) 48
X Hale pattern, No. 35, Mark I (rifle) 49
XI Newton pattern, No. 22, Mark I (rifle) 50
XII Smoke Bomb, No. 26 (P) 51
XIII Smoke Bomb, No. 27 (hand or rifle) 52
XIV Gas Bomb, No. 28 53
XV Signal Bomb, No. 31 (rifle), daylight 54
XVI Signal Bomb, No. 32, (rifle), night 55

GERMAN BOMBS.

XVII Stick Hand Bomb (time) 56
XVIII Use of Stick Bomb for firing Bangalore Torpedoes 58–59
XIX Egg Hand Bomb (time) 60
XX Smoke or Gas Hand Bomb (time) 61
XXI Automatic-lighting Stick Hand Bomb (time) ... 62
XXII Stick Hand Bomb (Percussion) 63
XXIII Rifle Bomb, 1913 64
XXIV Rifle Bomb, 1914 65
XXV Fuse Lighters 66
XXVI Bomb-throwers, 1915 and 1916 67
XXVII Stick Bomb 68

INTRODUCTORY NOTE.

Alterations in design and manufacture of bombs occur so frequently that it is impossible to include descriptions of all types which have, in the various stages of the war, been issued to the troops.

The bombs at present in use are dealt with in detail, but bombers must consider it one of their first duties to keep themselves acquainted with the numerous alterations in design which must inevitably take place from time to time as the result of experience and experiment.

Of the bombs described hereafter the Mills must be regarded as the most important, in that it is now both a hand and a rifle bomb, but all men of Bombing and Rifle-Bombing Sections should have a practical working knowledge of the Hale, Newton, egg, smoke and gas bombs, as far as possible.

This publication should not be quoted as an authority for supply, and demands should always be made in the official nomenclature ; thus, if a Mills bomb, No. 23, Mark II, is required, the demand should be for " grenade No. 23, Mark II."

INSTRUCTIONS ON BOMBING.
(PART I.)

CHAPTER I.

DESCRIPTION OF BRITISH BOMBS AND INSTRUC-
TIONS FOR THEIR USE.

MILLS BOMBS.
(a) *No. 5, Mark I* (*Hand*).
Weight filled, 1 lb. 6½ ozs.

(*See* Plate I.)

This is the original bomb of the type. It is still in use, but is no longer manufactured.

Description

Body.—Cast iron, segmented. Into one end is screwed a centre piece with separate cavities for the striker and the detonator.

The striker is kept cocked against the spring by its head engaging in the jaws of the striker lever, when the latter is lying against the body of the bomb ; the lever is retained in this position by the safety pin.

Igniter Set.—This consists of a cap, cap holder, safety fuze and N. 6 detonator.

Action.—On withdrawal of the safety pin the lever swings outwards under the pull of the striker spring, thus releasing the striker which fires the cap. The safety fuze burns for about 5 seconds and then fires the detonator.

Packing.—The bombs are packed 12 in a wooden box, with a tin containing 12 igniter sets and a key for removing the base plugs.

Range.—The bomb can be thrown by hand about 35 yards.

Inspection.—The following points should be noticed :—

(1) That there are two striking points at the lower end of the striker and not one central point ; a central point as used in Stokes Mortar Bombs may cause a premature explosion in a Mills Bomb.

(2) That the safety pin is not broken or badly corroded, and that the ends are correctly splayed, so that the pin cannot be jolted out, but yet is not too difficult to draw.

(3) That the jaws of the lever are in good condition, and support the striker correctly.

(4) That the wax seal round the top of the striker is unbroken.

(5) That the mouth of the detonator is closely crimped round the safety fuze ; that the fuze is in good condition and not cracked nor damaged by being bent ; that it is not loose in the cap, and that the cap has a central ventilating hole.

Instructions.

To prepare for use.—1. Unscrew the base and insert igniter set.

2. Screw home the base with the key provided.

To throw.—1. Hold the bomb in the right hand in such a position that the lever is held securely against the body of the bomb by the fingers.

2. Withdraw the safety pin with the left hand, using a hook if preferred, still keeping a firm grip on the lever.

3. Throw the bomb.

4. The lever must not be released before the bomb is thrown.

NOTE.—The prohibition against refilling bombs that have previously been used for dummy practice is particularly applicable to the Mills bomb.

(b) No. 23, Mark I (Rifle).

Weight filled complete with rod, 1 lb. 9¼ ozs.

This bomb is still in use, but is no longer manufactured.

Description

Body.—This is a No. 5 bomb fitted with a rod 5½ inches long, screwed into the base plug when the bomb is to be used as a rifle bomb. The bomb is issued with the hole in the base plug filled with a mixture of white lead and tallow to keep the threads from rusting.

Cup Attachment.—To keep the lever of the bomb in place after the safety pin has been withdrawn previous to firing, a ring attachment (*see* Plate II) is fixed to the rifle by means of the bayonet ; it is so constructed that it can be used with the long or short bayonet. This attachment cannot be used with the long rifle owing to the lack of distance between the bayonet and the bore of the rifle ; a special attachment is necessary in this case to take the place of the bayonet.

Cartridge.—43 grain blank cartridges will be used for this bomb and later marks with rods. The case of this cartridge is blackened.

Action.—When the rifle is fired the lever of the bomb is released as soon as it is clear of the cup attachment. The striker is thus released and the cap fired as in the No. 5.

Packing.—The wooden box contains 12 bombs, 12 igniter sets, 12 rods, 12 cartridges and key for base plug.

The handle cleats are painted white with letter " R " stencilled in black.

Range.—The mean maximum range, obtained by firing the rifle at an angle of elevation of 45° is 90 yards.

Instructions.—(Additional to those for No. 5.)

To prepare for use.—Screw the rod firmly into the base plug.

To fire.—1. Fix the cup attachment to the bayonet and fix the bayonet ; with long rifle, fix the special attachment.

2. Lower the rod into the rifle until the bomb is within the cup attachment, the lever being held by the ring.

3. Load the rifle with the special cartridge.

4. Immediately before firing, withdraw the safety pin.

Precautions.—(Additional to those for No. 5.)

1. See that the lever is securely held by the cup attachment against the body of the bomb.

2. Care must be taken that a cartridge with a bullet in it is not used.

3. The rod must be wiped clean of all oil before being placed in the rifle.

4. The base plug of the bomb should be steel or cast iron ; base plugs of other metals are liable to be penetrated by the rod.

No. 23, Mark II.

This only differs from the No. 23, Mark I, in the method of packing. It is still in use, but is no longer manufactured.

Packing.—The wooden box contains 12 bombs, 12 igniter sets, and a key for base plug.

The handle cleats are painted yellow with letter " R " stencilled in black.

The rods and cartridges are packed in a separate box which contains 120 rods and 130 cartridges. The ends of these boxes are painted yellow with " R C " stencilled in black.

No. 23, Mark III.

Weight filled complete with 6 in. rod, 1 lb. 5 ozs.

All components of this bomb differ slightly from those of the No. 23, Mark II, with the exception of the spring, safety pin, and igniter set.

(*See* Plate III.)

Description.

The body of the bomb is cast with a recess to receive the lever ; the lugs bearing the lever pivots are different in outline ; the striker has a slot in it and is supported by a square-ended flat lever fitting into the slot ; the filling hole is larger ; the centre piece is slightly shorter ; the base plug is slightly deeper.

Packing.—The arrangement, including painting of handle cleats, is the same as for the No. 23, Mark II.

(c) *No. 36, Mark I.*

Weight with disc, 1 lb. 8 ozs.

The body of the bomb is the same as that of the No. 23, Mark III, except that the base plug is flat.

(*See* Plate IV.)

Description.

Body.—A steel disc is screwed on to the base plug of the bomb, to fit inside the discharger (*see* Plate V) on the rifle and act as a gas check.

Igniter Set.—A special slow-burning safety fuze is used. It is buff-coloured, and is cut to burn for 7 seconds.

Cartridge.—A 30-grain Ballistite cartridge is used with this bomb. The top half of the case of this cartridge is blackened.

Packing.—The wooden box contains 12 bombs, 12 gas-checks, 12 7 seconds igniter sets, 14 Ballistite cartridges, and key for base plug. The handle cleats are painted pink with the letter " R " stencilled in black.

Method of Use.—1. The bomb is fired from the discharger described below. The shock of discharge is considerable so that the rifle must be fired from the kneeling position, with the butt of the rifle resting on the ground.

2. Having ascertained the range of the target, make the necessary adjustment to the gas port.

3. Open the breech of the rifle with the right hand and insert a round of the special blank ammunition supplied. Close the breech and pull back the safety catch.

4. Turn the rifle over so that the magazine is uppermost. Holding the rifle with the left hand at the nose cap, insert the bomb, disc downward, in the discharger until the safety pin is level with the rim. Pull out the safety pin with the index finger of the right hand, or with a bomber's hook.

Push the bomb down as far as it will go.

5. Gripping the rifle firmly with the left hand above the lower band, hold it at an angle of elevation of about 45°, the heel of the butt resting in a small hole in the ground previously made with the heel of the boot.

6. Push the safety catch forwards. Fire the rifle by pressing on the trigger with the index finger of the right hand.

CAUTION.—If the rifle is not fired at once it must on no account be pointed downwards so as to allow the bomb to drop out.

Range.—Mean maximum range, with the discharger about 210 yards.

BOMB DISCHARGERS.

Types of discharger for attachment to the short rifle, and to the 1914 pattern rifle are being introduced.

They are used for firing both the latest Mills pattern bombs and new patterns of smoke and signal bombs from the rifle without the use of a rod.

(a) *Bomb Discharger, S. & B. Pattern for Short M.L.E. Rifle.*

(*See* Plate V.)

Weight—2¼lbs.

Description.

The discharger consists of the following parts :—

1. The barrel into which the bomb is placed, and which has an adjustable gas port to enable variations in range to be made.

2. The base piece on to which this barrel can be screwed carrying two levers which fit into the slots of the nose cap **of** the rifle.

3. The central adjusting screw in this base for accurate centering and fitting on the muzzle of the rifle.

Instructions for Fitting.—Unscrew the adjusting screw until it is withdrawn upwards well clear of the base.

Place the base of the discharger on the top of the nose cap of the rifle so that the recess in the base fits against the bayonet boss, and with the forefinger and thumb of the left hand press the lever claws into the slots of the nose cap. Then screw down the barrel on to the base until it causes the levers to grip securely.

Then using a screw-driver screw down the adjusting screw inside the barrel just sufficiently to make contact with the muzzle of the rifle barrel.

If, before the barrel of the discharger is fully screwed down, the adjusting screw comes in contact with the end of the rifle barrel, the pressure of the levers will tend to force the nose of the cap off the rifle. For this reason the procedure detailed above must be invariably followed.

Owing to the fact that the length of the rifle barrel projecting through the nose cap is not the same in all rifles, the discharger when once fitted to a rifle should not be used with another, without refitting.

The adjusting screw should be removed, cleaned and re-adjusted to the rifle whenever an opportunity occurs, otherwise it will soon become so fixed by fouling that it will be impossible to unscrew it.

(b) Bomb Discharger S. & B. Pattern for 1914 Pattern Rifle.

The discharger is similar to that for the short rifle except that there is no adjusting screw, that the base is bored to fit over the end $\frac{5}{16}$ " of the muzzle of the barrel, and that the levers are longer so as to grip the barrel just below the block band foresight.

Egg Bomb No. 34, Mark III.

Weight Filled—11 oz.

(*See* Plate VI.)

Description.

Body.—Smooth cast iron egg shaped. Into one end is screwed a central tube to take the igniter, above this is screwed the concussion igniter consisting of striking chamber, with vent holes, and a striker, secured by means of copper shearing wire and safety pin with ring.

Igniter Set.—Consists of cap, cap holder, seven second fuse and No. 6 D detonator.

Action.—Withdraw the safety pin, tap the striker sharply on the heel of the boot, or a hard substance, thus firing the cap, and throw the bomb without delay.

Packing.—Bombs are packed 24 in a wooden box, with a tin containing 24 igniter sets, and a key for removing concussion igniter.

Instructions.—To prepare for use.

1. Unscrew the concussion igniter and insert igniter set.
2. Screw home the concussion igniter, using key to tighten.

Range.—Can be thrown with bent arm 50 to 60 yards.

Hale Pattern Rifle-Bombs.

(*a*) *No.* 3.

This was the original rifle-bomb of this type. It was fitted with a windvane which revolved during flight, releasing retaining bolts and so causing the bomb to arm. It is now obsolete.

(b) No. 20, Mark I.

Weight filled with rod, 1 lb. 6 oz.

This is still in use but is no longer manufactured.

Description.

Body.—Made of segmented steel, with a brass tube down the centre, into the forward end of which the detonator holder is inserted. The body of the bomb is closed by the base piece, carrying the striker pellet, two retaining bolts, the releasing socket, and a safety pin below the releasing socket.

Detonator Holder.—This consists of a brass tube which screws into the head of the bomb; it contains a detonator and percussion cap. When the detonator holder is not inserted, the head of the bomb is closed by an ebonite screw plug.

Rod.—This is 10 inches long.

Cartridges.—The 35-grain cordite cartridge is used.

Action.—On the shock of discharge, the releasing socket sets back, and the retaining bolts, no longer being held in position, fall out, leaving the striker pellet free to move forward. On impact, the striker pellet sets forward against the creep spring and fires the percussion cap.

Packing.—The wooden box provided contains 20 bombs, four tins each with five detonator holders, and a separate tin containing 22 cartridges.

Range.—The mean maximum range is 220 yards.

Inspection.—The following points should be noticed :—

(1) That the releasing socket and safety pin are correctly in place.

(2) That the striker pellet is correctly held by the retaining bolts, and that the creep spring is in position over the striker pellet.

(3) That the cavity for the detonator holder is clean.

(4) That the rod is straight and clean, and free from oil.

(5) That the metal at the lower end of the detonator holder is correctly turned in over the percussion cap, so that the latter is securely held ; otherwise, the cap may set back on the shock of discharge and cause a premature.

Instructions.

To Prepare for Use.—1. Remove the ebonite screw plug and tap the bomb, head downwards, on the palm of the hand to ensure that the striker pellet is properly held in place by the retaining bolts.

2. Screw in the detonator holder.

To Fire.—1. Lower the rod into the barrel of the rifle.

2. Load the rifle with the special cartridge.

3. Immediately before firing, withdraw the safety pin.

Precautions.

1. The releasing socket must not be tampered with.

2. After withdrawing the safety pin it should be noticed whether the releasing socket is still in its right position ; it may slip back, thus releasing the retaining bolts, if in manufacture it has not been properly secured over the retaining rim. A bomb in this condition is dangerous, and would probably explode prematurely at the muzzle of the rifle.

3. The bomb must not be fired with a cartridge containing a bullet.

(b) No. 20, Mark II.

This is still in use, but is no longer manufactured. It has a different cap (·162 percussion) in the detonator, a circumferentially grooved body of steel tubing, and a blunt striker (*see* Plate VII), and the explosive is contained in a waxed paper cartridge.

(c) No. 24, Mark I.

The bomb is still in use, but is no longer manufactured. It is a modified form of No. 20, from which it differs in the following particulars :—

Weight filled without rod, 1 lb. 2 oz.

(*See* Plate VIII.)

Description.

Body.—Steel, circumferentially grooved. The releasing socket is 1 inch long instead of $1\frac{3}{4}$ inches, and the brass base is correspondingly shorter. The lower end of the base is not belled so that the brass sleeve drops off about 10 yards from the rifle. The rod is 10 inches in length.

The striker is $\frac{1}{2}$ inch shorter and the point is blunt.

The brass gaine tube in the centre of the body is shortened, so that only the end of the detonator holder engages in it, whereas in No. 20 the tube comes right up to the top of the body.

Detonator Holder.—The detonator holder is 2 inches long instead of 2⅝ inches, and its milled top is a sleeve instead of turned out of the solid.

Packing.—Each box contains 20 bombs complete with 22 cartridges.

Range.—The mean maximum range is 280 yards.

(c) *No.* 24, *Mark II.*
(*See* Plate IX.)

This is similar to No. 24, Mark I, except that :—
Weight filled with 15-inch rods is 1 lb. 7 oz.

Description.

Body.—(*a*) The body is plain and is made of cast iron.

(*b*) The closing plug in the head of the bomb is made of die cast metal.

(*c*) A proportion of the supply is fitted with 15-inch rods, and the remainder with 11-inch rods.

Range with 11-inch rod 220 yards.

  „   „ 15 „   „ 350 „

Packing.—Each box contains 20 bombs complete with 22 cartridges.

(d) *No.* 35, *Mark I.*

Weight complete, 1 lb. 5 ozs. filled and with 15-inch rod.

(*See* Plate X.)

Description.

The bomb is similar to the No. 24, Mark II with the following differences in construction :—

Body.—The explosive charge as before is contained in a waxed paper cylinder closed at each end by a waxed cardboard disc. The body is closed at the top by a brass screw and at the lower end by a brass plug which carries the retaining bolts, &c., as in the No. 24. The length of the base plug is 1 inch long and is completely covered by the brass retaining sleeve, the safety pin passing through the sleeve instead of immediately beneath it.

Detonator holder.—This consists of a capped cartridge case with four ¼-inch holes near the lower end, the flange is turned off and a cover is placed over the end to secure the percussion cap. The cartridge case contains a 3·05 grain detonator surrounded with paper.

Rod.—A proportion of the supply is fitted with 15-inch rods, and the remainder with 11-inch rods.

Cartridge.—The 43-grain cordite cartridge will be used.

Action.—The same as in Nos. 20, 24, Marks I and II.

Packing.—Each box contains 20 bombs, one tin box containing 22 blank cartridges and 2 tin boxes containing 10 detonators each.

Range.—Mean maximum :—

With 15-inch rod, 350 yards, and with 11-inch rod, 220 yards.

Inspection.—As in Nos. 20, 24, Marks I and II.

Precautions.—As in Nos. 20, 24, Marks I and II.

NEWTON PATTERN RIFLE-BOMB.

(a) *Locally Made Pattern.*

Description.

Very similar to the No. 22 described below. The rod was 17½ inches long with a gas check. This pattern is now obsolete.

(b) *No. 22, Mark I.*

Weight filled with 15-inch rod, 1 lb. 9¼ oz.
(*See* Plate XI.)

Description.

This is still in use, but is no longer manufactured.

Body.—Of segmented cast iron with a flat head and having four projections cast on. In the centre of the flat head is a hole in which is inserted and fixed a waxed millboard tube with the lower end closed, to take the special detonator set.

Cover.—Over the upper end of the bomb is placed a detachable pressed steel cover with four slotted lugs fitting over the four projections cast on the side of the bomb. The striker is rivetted in the centre of the cover.

Detonator Set.—This consists of an ordinary capped ·303 cartridge case inside which is a paper tube containing a No. 8 detonator (open end towards the cap). A tin shield is placed over the cap to prevent the cover setting back on shock of discharge and firing the cap at the muzzle ; it must not be removed.

Rod.—This is 15-inches long, with a gas check.

Cartridges.—The 43-grain cartridge will be used in future.

Action.—On contact with the ground the striker inside the cover pierces both the tin shield and the cap, causing the detonator to explode.

Packing.—Each box contains 12 bombs, a large tin box holding 12 detonator sets, a small tin box holding 13 blank cartridges and a steel key to remove covers.

Range.—Mean maximum range 350 yards.

Inspection.—The following points should be noticed :—

    (1) That the lugs on the caps fit snugly over the projections on the body.

    (2) That the tin shield is in place.

    (3) That the rod is wiped clean of all oil and dirt.

Instructions.

To prepare for use :—

    (1) Remove cover with key and insert detonator set, without removing tin shield over cap.

    (2) Replace cover and see that projections on bomb pass through slots in lugs of cover.

    (3) Lower the rod of the bomb into the barrel of the rifle.

    (4) Load rifle with special cartridge.

SMOKE BOMB.

(a) P. Bomb, No. 26.

Weight complete, 1 lb. 6 oz.

(*See* Plate XII.)

Description.

Body.—Consists of a tin cylinder 3 inches diameter and 5 inches long. In one end is soldered a detonator tube and a short length of copper wire for binding purposes. The cylinder is filled with red phosphorus.

Detonator.—This is an ordinary No. 8 fitted with a 9-seconds fuze and Brock lighter.

Action.—The bomb when exploded produces a thick white smoke, the phosphorus thrown out causes burns and may cause fires.

Packing.—Twelve bombs in a box, which also contains a tin of 12 detonators, fuzes, and fuze lighters and two brassards.

Instructions.

To Prepare for Use.—Insert the detonator in detonator tube and bind in place with copper wire.

Precautions.

Wherever stored, the bombs should be examined from time to time to see that the tins have not become corroded or rusted through into holes, as there is a danger of fire when the red phosphorus is exposed to the atmosphere.

(b) No. 27 Bomb, Hand or Rifle.

Weight, 1 lb. 4 oz. without rod.

(*See* Plate XIII.)

Description.

Body.—The bomb consists of a cylindrical tin canister, filled with white phosphorus.

In the top end is soldered a brass spigot, screwed on the outside ; into this is soldered a brass or copper gaine tube to take the detonator, &c.

To the lower end is soldered a steel disc tapped in the centre, into which screws the rod for the rifle.

Concussion Igniter.—This consists of a solid brass striker pellet $\frac{3}{4}$ inch long and $\frac{7}{16}$ inch diameter with a single centre striker at one end. The pellet fits into a small brass tube with a shoulder half way down, the lower end of which screws on to the brass spigot on the body of the bomb. In the lower part of this tube is a hole for gas escape.

Through this brass tube and the striker, a hole is drilled to take the shearing wire, the ends of which are brought round and twisted together. A safety cap is provided which consists of another brass tube closed at the top $1\frac{3}{4}$ inches long by

$\frac{5}{8}$ inch diameter fitting over the striker and striker holder. Through this and through the striker pellet, is another hole for the safety pin.

Burster, &c.—This consists of a ·410 centre fire cap having paper-covered side ventilation holes and a 6½-second fuze to the other end of which is attached a No. 3 detonator.

Rod.—This is 15 inches long.

Cartridge.—The 43-grain cartridge will be used.

Action.—On the shock of discharge when used as a rifle-bomb the inertia of the striker pellet breaks the shearing wire, and the striker hits the cap, which lights the fuze. On bursting, the bomb gives off dense white clouds and burning phosphorus is scattered, which causes burns and may cause fires.

Packing.—The bombs are packed 12 in a box. In a separate box are packed 48 15-inch rods and 48 cartridges. In a third box are packed 144 detonating sets or bursters.

Precautions.

The precautions as regards storage already described for the No. 26 P. bomb are still more important in the case of this bomb, since white phosphorus instantly takes fire on contact with air.

Mean Maximum Range.—240 yards.

Inspection.—Remove the safety pin and cap and make quite certain that the shearing wire is in place and unbroken.

Instructions.

To Prepare for Use.—1. Insert the detonator.

2. Screw the striker set on to the spigot in the top of the bomb.

3. When required as a rifle-bomb, screw in the rod well home.

4. Wipe rod clean of all oil and dirt.

To fire.—1. Lower the rod into the rifle.

2. Load the rifle with special blank cartridge.

3. Immediately before firing, remove the safety pin and take off the safety cap.

To Use as a Hand Bomb.—1. Remove the safety pin and cap.

2. Strike the head of the striker pellet on the heel of the boot or some other hard surface, and throw the bomb without delay.

(c) *New Design.*

A new design for use with the discharger having similar body but with a steel gas-check soldered to the base in lieu of a rod is being introduced.

GAS BOMBS, No. 28.

Weight complete, 2 lbs.

(*See* Plate XIV.)

Description.

Body.—This is of cast iron, shaped like a ball, with a 1-inch tapped hole into which screws the cast iron detonator holder; this has a screwed nipple at the top end.

Striker Set.—This is similar to the concussion igniter of No. 27 bomb.

Packing.—Each box contains 12 bombs complete with 12 the igniters or bursters.

Detonator set or Burster.—This is similar to that described for the No. 27 bomb except that the fuze is 5 seconds and a No. 8 commercial detonator is used.

Inspection.—Remove the safety cap and ascertain whether the shearing wire is intact.

Instructions.

To Prepare for Use.—1. Unscrew the striker set.

2. Insert the detonator with fuze, &c.

3. Screw on the striker set.

To Throw.—1. Withdraw the safety pin.

2. Remove the cap.

3. Strike the head of the striker pellet on the heel of the boot or some other hard surface, and throw the bomb without delay.

SIGNAL BOMBS.

(a) *No.* 31—*Rifle Bomb* (*Daylight Signal*).
Weight complete, 1 lb. 4 oz.

(*See* Plate XV.)

Description.

Body.—This is a tin cylinder, with a screwed brass boss or spigot soldered on the top and to take the striker set.

Inside the body at the top end is a felt wad, upon the upper surface of which the black powder bursting charge is pasted. The ends of the quick match connecting with the smoke candle are passed through the central hole of the felt washer and laid over the bursting charge. Next is a millboard cylinder containing smoke-producing compound round the top portion of which the tapes of quick match are bound by string. The lower portion of the millboard cylinder is covered by a linen bag which is gummed on. Between the millboard cylinder and the parachute there is cotton wool packing and a millboard disc, at the side of which passes the string connecting the smoke container to the parachute. The parachute is rolled round a millboard stick in the lower end of the body.

Striker Set, &c.—This is similar to the concussion igniter of the No. 27 bomb already described, but it is not used for ignition by hand.

Action.—On the shock of discharge, the inertia of the striker pellet breaks the shearing wire, and the striker hits the cap which lights the fuze. There is no detonator attached ; the fuze lights the bursting charge direct. The bomb is timed to burst at its attached maximum height and the signal is supported in the air by the parachute.

Packing.—The bombs are packed 12 in a box complete with 15 inch rods, 13 cartridges in a tin box, and 12 igniters in a cylinder.

(b) No. 32 Rifle-Bomb (Night Signal).

This is the same as No. 31, but instead of containing smoke-producing compound it contains stars for night signals. (*See* Plate XVI.)

(c) New Design.

A new design for use with the discharger having a similar body, but with a steel gas-check soldered to the base in lieu of a rod is being introduced.

Bomb Cartridges.

(a) *Ballistite.*

(For use with dischargers.)

Description.

The cartridge contains 30 grains of sporting Ballistite with a tuft of plain cotton wool filled in the neck, above which is a glazed board disc sealed with shellac. Half of the case is blackened with bronzing liquid.

(b) *43-grain, Mark II.*

(For use with rifle bombs. With rods).

Description.

The cartridge is loaded with about 43 grain of special M.D.-cordite and has a guncotton tuft above and below the charge. The top is closed with a shellacked paper disc and there is no filling of either wax or tallow in the neck. The case is blackened with bronzing liquid.

(c) *35-grain (Hales pattern cartridge.)*

Description.

This cartridge is still under restricted manufacture, but its use is mainly confined to rifle-bombs having 11-inch rods.

It is loaded with 35 grains of $3\frac{3}{4}$ cordite and has gun cotton tufts above and below the charge. The top is closed with a cordite disc and a shellacked paper disc.

The neck was originally filled with tallow, but this has been discontinued and the space is now left empty.

The case is of plain brass.

CHAPTER II.

DESCRIPTION OF GERMAN BOMBS AND IN-STRUCTIONS FOR THEIR USE.

German Policy.

According to " *Nahkampfmittel* " (" Weapons of Close Combat "), 1st January, 1917, the German official manual an abbreviated translation of which was issued as S.S. 562 :— " At the present moment all the hand bombs used in the German Army are time bombs." In the text of this manual only two bombs are mentioned : the " Stick " (*Stielhandgranate*) and Egg (*Eierhandgranate*). It is very exceptional that any bombs but these two and the smoke and gas hand bombs are found on the battlefield, or in the enemy's possession. A modification of the ordinary " Stick " bomb has recently been noticed (Plate XXI) : it has a device by which the safety fuze is lighted automatically after the missile has left the thrower's hand. In a document captured in June, 1917, it is stated that :—" A stick hand bomb, the fuze of which burns only 2—3 seconds (instead of $5\frac{1}{2}$) has been already tried successfully and will shortly be introduced. This combines the advantages of a percussion and a time hand bomb."

The bombs that need to be known most thoroughly are those shown on Plates XVII, XIX, and XX.

Improvised hand bombs are still occasionally picked up. The types of igniters used in them are described and illustrated. (*See* page 33 and Plate XXV.)

It is stated in " *Nahkampfmittel* " that the manufacture of rifle-bombs has been discontinued, as owing to their want of accuracy their value is very doubtful, but as they are still in use, descriptions of them are included. Their place is being taken by the " Stick " bombs fired from a bomb thrower. (Plate XXVII).

According to a German document, dated August 17, 1917, a new rifle-bomb similar to the French bomb is being introduced.

Precautions (General).

The following *precautions* should be taken with any bombs that may be found or captured :—

(1) The bombs should be examined at once by a trained bomber, in order to find out whether they are live, how they are fired, &c.

(2) The means of firing will probably be immediately apparent to a trained bomber, but during examination bombs should be handled with care.

(3) A man who does not understand bombs should not touch them, but should report the presence of a store of bombs to the nearest bomber, N.C.O. or officer. Treading near percussion hand bombs, and stick hand bombs with the cap removed and the firing string hanging out, should be avoided. Percussion bombs that are blind or from which the safety pin has been removed should be destroyed *in situ*.

(4) When used against the enemy, a bomb should be thrown as soon as it is "lit," even if there is no apparent evidence of the fuze burning.

(5) Arrangements for removing, storing or destroying bombs found in a captured position should be made as soon as possible by bombing officers.

(6) Bombing officers will also be responsible that, when samples of bombs are taken back to headquarters for examination, the bombs are not in a dangerous condition, and the detonators have been removed.

Stick Hand Bomb (Time).

(Cylindrical Hand Bomb with Handle.)

(*Stielhandgranate B.Z.*).

Weight, 1 lb. 13 oz.

(*See* Plate XVII, Figs. 1 and 2.)

Description.

Body.—Tin cylinder, containing a cartridge of from 7 to 10 oz. of explosive. The exterior dimensions of the cylinder vary approximately from 3¾ inches long by 2¼ inches diameter to 4½ inches long by 2¾ inches diameter.

The **top** is closed by a lid held in place by four clips or lapped over ; at the bottom there is a screw-threaded hole to take the handle. The cartridge is fitted with a paper tube for the detonator. On the side of the body there is a hook, by means of which the bomb can be attached to the belt.

The inscription on the body, " *Vor Gebrauch Sprengkapsel einsetzen* " means " Before use insert the detonator."

Handle.—Wooden, about 9 inches long, with a metal top screwed to fit the body. It is bored axially to take the igniter and wire pull, and has a hollow formed in its end covered by a screwed metal cover. On removal of this cover a string loop coiled up, with a porcelain button, will be found. The string is attached to the wire pull. In the early patterns of the bomb there was no button or screwed cover, and the string loop was turned up the handle and fastened to it by means of a paper band. When the handle is unscrewed from the body, in its head will be seen a brass tube from which the detonator projects.

Method of Ignition.—The means of ignition consists of a friction lighter contained in a cardboard tube set in action by pulling the string to which the wire pull is attached, and a length of safety fuze which burns 5½ or 7 seconds (as marked on the handle)*, with a dab of phosphorus on the end. The mouth of the detonator faces the phosphorus.

Safety Arrangements.—1. The bomb and detonator are kept separate during carriage.

2. The string loop is contained in a metal cover. This cover should only be removed just before firing.

Instructions.

To prepare for use.—1. Unscrew the handle and see if the detonator is in position ; if it is, refix the handle.

2. Hold the bomb in the right hand.

3. With the left hand unscrew the metal cover.

4. Pull the loop or button with the left hand.

5. Throw immediately.

---

* It is possible that bombs burning only 2 or 3 seconds may be found as they have been mentioned in a captured document.

If the detonator is not in position, search should be made for a supply of the proper detonators. Fit the mouth of the detonator into the projecting brass tube, screw in the handle, and then proceed as in 2, 3, 4 and 5 above.

To render safe.—1. Unscrew the handle and remove the detonator.

2. Pull the string loop, which will light the fuze, and throw the handle away.

NOTE.—The red bomb found in some boxes is a dummy for instructional purposes, without fuze, detonator or exploder.

NOTE.—The stick hand bomb is made use of for several purposes besides throwing as a missile :—

    (*a*) For ignition of " Bangalore " torpedoes. (*See* Plate XVIII, Figs. 1, 2 and 3.)

    (*b*) For charges for demolitions, both long and concentrated. (*See* Plate XVIII, Figs. 4 and 5.)

    (*c*) For demolition of guns.

CAUTION.—There are two other patterns of stick bombs. They are described below :—

    (*a*) The automatic lighting stick hand bomb (time). This has a metal handle. (*See* p. 12).

    (*b*) The stick hand bomb (percussion), of which a few specimens have been found. This requires to be handled with care. It is distinguishable by the half of the handle nearer the charge being metal. (*See* p. 13.)

EGG HAND BOMB (TIME).

(*Eierhandgranate.*)

Weight, 11 oz. (but patterns vary slightly).
Can be thrown about 50 yards.

(*See* Plate XIX.)

Description.

Body.—Cast iron, egg-shaped, about 60 mm. (2·3 inches) long by 45 mm. (1·77 inches) diameter, with a screwed hole at one end to receive the igniter. It is filled with a special powder which does not require a detonator.

Method of Ignition.—The igniter, which is operated by pulling a wire loop either by hand or by a wrist strap, is described under Fuze Lighters (page 33). It makes a particularly loud crack when pulled.

Safety Arrangements.—The igniter is carried separate from the bomb; a small lead plug is screwed into the body and must be removed before the igniter can be inserted.

Instructions.

To prepare for use.—1. Unscrew and remove the lead plug. 2. Screw in the igniter.

It is important when screwing in the igniter to keep the bomb upright, so that no powder can get into the screw threads.

To throw.—Pull the wire loop either by hand or by a wrist strap and throw in the usual way.

To render safe.—Unscrew the igniter, and replace it by a plug. If necessary, empty out the powder.

Smoke Hand Bomb (Time).

(*Hand-Nebelbombe.*)

Weight, about 2 lbs.

(*See* Plate XX.)

Description.

This bomb produces a fairly dense white cloud intended to hide movement, and drive men out of dug-outs and shelters. It has no unpleasant effects in the open air.

Body.—Spherical, (3·9) inches in diameter, filled with about 21 to 23 oz. of "*N. Stoff.*" It is formed of two hemispheres of tin plate, ·04-in. thick, united by a lapped-over joint at the equator. There are two openings, situated at the ends of a diameter perpendicular to the plane of the joint. One is for filling and is closed with a lead washer and hexagonal nut. The other has a gaine $2\frac{1}{2}$ inches deep, closed by a screw plug and containing a small charge of black powder. Before use, the plug is removed and a friction lighter is inserted.

The bomb is painted field-grey, and has the word "*Neb l*" stencilled on it.

Method of Ignition.—The friction lighter is fired by pulling out the wire in the direction of the axis of the tube. Time of burning, 5 or 6 seconds, according to the pattern. The head of the 5-seconds fuze is painted red.

Safety Arrangements.—1. The bomb and friction lighter are kept separate during carriage.

2. To prevent an accidental direct pull on the friction lighter the wire loop is bent over.

Instructions.

To prepare for use.—1. Take the friction lighter and remove the oiled paper from the gas escape holes, straighten the wire loop, taking care not to pull it.

2. Remove the plug from the gaine and insert the lighter, taking care that the bomb is upright, so that no powder in the gaine can get into the thread of the screw.

3. Pull the loop of the lighter.

4. Throw the bomb.

The bomb can be fired, by means of a special holder, from a rifle, or thrown by a catapult. In either case the longer fuze is used.

Precautions.—1. " *N. Stoff* " must not be allowed to come into contact with a friction lighter or detonator, as it will explode them.

2. The bomb must be thrown at least 20 yards to prevent inconvenience from the smoke or fragments of tin plate.

To render safe.—Unscrew the lighter, and if necessary shake out the black powder.

Gas Hand Bomb C (Time).

(*Handgasbombe C.*)

Description.

These bombs are exactly similar in appearance to the smoke hand bomb (see Plate XX), except that they have " *Gas C* " stencilled on them in red, instead of the word " *Nebel.*"

They are filled with a liquid (methyl-sulphuric-chloride) and a few small shot. Weight, about 1¾ lbs.

The contents are intended to attack the eyes and lungs, and the bombs are used for clearing trenches and saps. The gas is said, " according to the strength of the wind, to remain effective 30 minutes."

Instructions for use, method of rendering useless, &c., are the same as for the smoke hand bomb, with the following additional *Precautions* :—

(1) Unless the wind is very suitable, it is better to fire the bomb from a rifle than to throw it.

(2) The bombs should, if possiblé, be kept in the open, as the vapour from them in a confined space is dangerous.

(3) Damaged bombs should be buried, the materials in which they are packed burnt, and the cases scrubbed.

AUTOMATIC-LIGHTING STICK HAND BOMB (TIME).

(*See* Plate XXI.)

Description.

This bomb is similar in appearance to the ordinary "stick" hand bomb, except that the handle is of metal painted field grey instead of being of wood.

Method of Ignition.—In the hollow handle is a cylindrical weight, attached by a wire, part of which is coiled, to the friction lighter. Safety fuze and detonator are arranged as in the ordinary "Stick" bomb. When the screw cap at the end of the stick is removed, the weight is free to slide out, and when it does so, it pulls the wire and sets the friction lighter in action. Thus the bomb is lighted in the act of throwing.

Safety Arrangements.—1. The bomb and detonator are kept separate during carriage.

2. The firing weight is retained by the screw cap.

Instructions.

To Prepare for Use.—1. Unscrew the handle, and see if the detonator is in position ; insert it if not already there and refix the handle.

2. Hold the bomb in the right hand and unscrew the screw cap at the end of the stick.

3. Throw the bomb well into the air.

To Render Safe.—After making sure that the screw cap is in position and the weight is not loose, unscrew the handle and remove the detonator.

STICK HAND BOMB (PERCUSSION).

(*See* Plate XXII.)

Description.

This bomb is almost exactly similar in general outward appearance to the stick bomb (time). The only external difference is that the upper end of the stick is metal, not wood. When the cap at the end of the handle is removed no string and metal will be found. The hole down the centre of the wooden handle is much larger than in the "time" pattern.

The handle screws off and charge and detonator are arranged as in the "time" bomb.

Method of Ignition.—The percussion mechanism consists of a cap holder and striker pellet with needle. The striker pellet is held in the safe position by two cylindrical knobs on the ends of a hairpin spring. This spring is kept compressed and the knobs therefore are held in the grooves in the striker pellet by a sleeve. This sleeve is weighted at the end furthest away from the head and kept in position by a screw cap. When the cap is removed and the bomb thrown the weighted sleeve falls out; this releases the spring and leaves the pellet free to strike the cap. As the ends of the cap holder and the striker pellet, and their seatings, are coned, the striker is driven into the cap, on whichever side the bomb falls.

Safety Arrangements.—None beyond the screw cover above described.

Instructions.

To Use.—1. Unscrew the cover.

2. Throw in such a way that the bomb turns over and over in the air, and that the motion may cause the sleeve to fall out.

To Render Safe.—If the screw cover has not been removed, unscrew the handle and remove the detonator as with the stick hand bomb (time).

NOTE.—Blinds or bombs from which the sleeve has been removed are dangerous and should be destroyed without being touched.

RIFLE BOMB, 1913.   PERCUSSION.

Weight, about 2 lbs. complete.   Charge, 3·2 oz. explosive.

Maximum mean range—350 yards.

(*See* Plate XXIII.)

Description.

Body.—Steel, 4·3 inches long and ·16 inch thick, is serrated longitudinally and transversely, so that on detonation it may split up into fragments of sufficient size.   It is painted grey. The base is closed by a brass base cup, which has screwed into it a steel tail rod 18 inches long, with copper gas check to take the grooves of the rifling.   The rod has a thin coating of copper to protect it from rust, and also to protect the barrel.   A tin disc is fastened to the head of the bomb, by the igniter plug, for short ranges.

Method of Ignition.—An igniter plug, carrying cap and detonator, screwed into the head of the bomb.   A brass tube passing through the centre of the bomb contains a striker pellet, with needle and creep spring.

Safety Arrangements.—1. A powder safety device is contained in base cup.   Screwed into the striker pellet is a spindle, which passes through into the base cup, and has at its lower end a small platform with three flash-holes.   On this rests a pellet of compressed powder, the object of which is to keep the striker from moving forward until a short time after the bomb has left the rifle.   This powder is ignited by means of a small brass pellet with a cap, which sets back on the shock of discharge, and compressing a small spring, is penetrated by a needle on the screw plug closing the base cup. A vent hole in the base cup allows the escape of the gases of combustion.   This is normally sealed with wax.

2. When the powder is burnt away, the striker is only prevented from moving forward by a creep spring, the resistance of which is overcome on strike.

Instructions.

To Use.—1. Unscrew the zinc plug from the head.

2. Screw in the igniter plug (with tin disc for ranges under 200 yards).

3. Lower the bomb carefully into the barrel.

4. Insert a rifle-bomb cartridge in the breech.

5. Fix the rifle at the required elevation.

6. Fire the rifle.

To Render Safe.—Unscrew the igniter plug in the head of the bomb, holding the bomb with the rod downward.

Precautions.—1. A German rifle 98 or 88'05 only can be used.

2. Care must be taken that the bomb is not dropped, especially on the tail rod, as then it is liable to become "live," and will therefore detonate on firing. It should be carried head uppermost by the bomb, not by the rod.

3. The special rifle-bomb cartridge must be used, and in no case a ball cartridge.

4. Tail rods which jam or rub when being placed in the barrel must not be used, and no force is to be employed.

5. Damp tail rods should be dried before use. All rods should be firmly screwed in.

NOTE.—An improved pattern of the 1913 Rifle-bomb has been noticed. It is provided with a two-pronged safety pin like the 1914 pattern, but inserted in the brass base in order to hold the striker pellet from moving. This safety pin must be removed before firing.

The following warning is also given :—

" After taking the bomb from the box it should be examined to see that the gas escape hole is closed and has not been blackened by the burning of the powder pellet. Bombs in which this has happened are dangerous and must not be used.'

RIFLE BOMB, 1914. PERCUSSION.

(*Gewehrgranate.*)

Weight, about 2 lbs.
Maximum mean range—380 yards.

(*See* Plate XXIV.)

Description.

Body.—Cast iron, 0·2 inch thick, painted field gray, and serrated to give fragments of sufficient size on detonation. The charge (2¾ oz.) is made up in a thin cardboard cylinder, which is retained in the bomb by a shoulder piece screwing on to the body. The nose of the bomb is screw-threaded to take the percussion fuze, and the base to take a nipple for a tin disc and tail rod with gas check. Until the fuze is inserted the nose is protected from dust and damp by a plug and leather washer.

Method of Ignition.—The percussion fuze contains an exploding charge with detonator and cap. The last named is set off by a striker pellet screwed into the socket of the fuze. The needle of the pellet is hinged and lies flat on top of the cap when in the safety position, but is pulled and maintained erect by the spring in the striker pellet as soon as the pellet moves forward after firing.

Safety Arrangements.—1. The striker pellet is retained in position by a locking ball which rests in a recess in the pellet. This ball is prevented from falling out by a locking ring which is held by a flat spring with curved ends. On the rifle being fired the locking ring overcomes the spring and sets back, and the locking ball is driven out of its recess by the striker pellet, which, acting under the pressure of its spring, moves forward out of the body together with the nose of the fuze. At the same time the needle pellet spring pulls up the needle into the firing position.

2. The striker pellet is prevented by its spring from being driven back on to the cap until impact.

Instructions.

To Use.—1. Unscrew the plug by means of the key, pull the two-pronged safety pin from the fuze and screw the fuze in slowly and carefully by means of the key.

2. Lower the bomb carefully into the barrel.

3. Insert the special cartridge in the breech.

4. Fix the rifle at the required elevation.

5. Fire the rifle.

To Render Safe.—Unscrew the fuze from the bomb. (*See* Precaution 2.)

Precautions.—1. A German rifle, 98 or 88'05, only can be used.

2. Care must be taken after the fuze has been inserted that the bomb is not dropped, especially on the tail rod, as then it is liable to become " live," and will therefore detonate on

firing. It should be carried head uppermost by the bomb, not by the rod.

3. The special rifle-bomb cartridge must be used, and in no case a ball cartridge.

4. Tail rods which jam or rub when being placed in the barrel must not be used, and no force is to be employed.

5. Damp tail rods should be dried before use. All rods should be firmly screwed in.

Warning.

Bombs with live fuzes should not be fired or touched; they are easily recognisable, as the nose of the fuze will be found sticking out (compare Figs. 1 and 2). Bombs in this condition and blinds should be destroyed as soon as possible.

Once the fuze has been screwed in the bomb must be handled with caution, *vide* Precaution 2.

FUZE LIGHTERS.

(*Used with certain Service and Improvised Hand Bombs and Mobile Charges.*)

(*See* Plate XXV.)

1. *Brass Spring Fuze Lighter (Sprengpatronzünder).* (*See* Fig. 1.)

This consists of a spring, striker and cap, encased in a brass tube in prolongation of which is a smaller tube to receive the end of the safety fuze.

The spring is compressed by a collar at the end of the striker rod. The rod is held back by a safety pin passing through it at the end of the case.

To Fire.—Withdraw the pin ; the striker then flies forward and fires the cap, thus lighting the fuze.

This spring lighter is used in most of the German extemporised hand bombs, land mines, charges for destroying dug-outs, etc. It is usually fastened in position by a staple.

The fuze employed burns about an inch in three seconds.

2. *Friction Lighter.* (*See* Figs. 2 and 3.)

This is a combination of friction tube, lighter and fuze. It consists of a lead alloy tube from which a wire loop projects. It has a screw thread cut on its surface for securing it in a bomb.

The wire has a friction bar on it surrounded by a friction composition and below this is sufficient slow burning powder to fire, in one pattern five seconds, in another seven seconds. The head of the five seconds lighter is painted red.

To Fire.—Pull the wire loop.

This lighter is used in the egg hand-bombs. A somewhat similar lighter (*See* Fig. 3) is used in the smoke and gas hand bombs, and in the spherical hand bomb.

3. *Match-head Fuze Lighter.* (*See* Fig. 4.)

This consists of a small lead tube, $\frac{7}{8}''$ long, closed at one end with a ball of red phosphorus, varnished and covered with oiled paper. Safety fuze can be inserted at the other end and secured by crimping the lead tube round it.

To Fire.—Tear off the paper from the lighter and rub the match head with some rough material (*e.g.* side of match box).

BOMB-THROWERS 1915 AND 1916.

(*a*) *The* 1915 *Pattern Bomb-Thrower* ("*Granatwerfer* 15") *for Stick-Bomb* ("*Wurfgranate*").

1. *The Bomb-Thrower.*—(Plate XXVI, Fig. 1) consists of the bomb-thrower proper and the bed-plate.

The bomb-thrower is made up of the following parts :— "Stick," clinometer, trunnions, traversing arc and base plate.

The bed plate, of sheet iron, has a semi-circular flange underneath to absorb the recoil ; the flange should be well sunk into the ground. On the bed plate is riveted a semi-circular collar, in which the bomb-thrower is held by two clamping screws.

With the bomb-thrower is also a case containing tools and spare parts.

2. *The* 1915 *Pattern Stick-Bomb* (*Wurfgranate 15*), as shown in Plate XXVII, consists of the body (chilled cast-iron), 4-winged shaft, containing cartridge, percussion fuze, detonator (2.5 g. fulminate), gaine, and charge (225 g. safety explosive).

3. *The Fuze.*—When the tape has been freed and the safety pin (para. 9) removed, the percussion pellet is only kept away from the percussion cap by the creep spring.

On impact, the inertia of the pellet carries it forward. The creep spring is compressed and the striker hits the percussion cap. The flashes pass through the holes in the percussion pellet, into the powder pellet, ignites the latter and fires the detonator, which in turn detonates the charge.

4. *To Prepare the Bomb for Use.*—Unscrew the fuze, insert a detonator, screw in the fuze, and, if necessary, straighten bent wings with the flat-nose pliers.

5. *Packing of Stick Bombs.*—One case contains 10 stick-bombs, with percussion fuze screwed in and blank cartridge inserted, and 10 detonators in a special waterproof box.

To Cock and Set to Safety.—Press down the cocking collar until the firing hook catches. Turn down the safety catch until the letter S (*Sicherung*=safety) is visible.

7. *Laying for Line.*—After loosening the clamp screws, bring the traversing arc to the point required by turning it on the base plate, and clamp it tight.

8. *Laying for Elevation.*—Set the pointer of the water level to the degree corresponding to the range (*see* Range Table below), then adjust the level by raising or lowering the " stick " and clamp the latter.

9. *Loading.*—Place the bomb with its shaft on the " stick." On the word " Ready," free the tape on the safety pin, and remove this pin.

Turn the firing lever in the direction from which firing is to be carried out, and hook on the lanyard.

10. *Firing* —Turn up the safety catch until the letter F (*Feuer*=Fire) is visible. Take cover.

To Fire. Release the firing lever by giving the lanyard a smart jerk.

11. *Precautions.*—Always fire with the lanyard, and from under cover.

Should the bomb not be fired, replace the safety pin, fasten the tape, and only then withdraw the bomb from the " stick."

Bombs should not be carried about with the detonators in them.

Firing should not take place at ranges of less than 55 yards to avoid endangering our own troops.

12. *To Dismount the " Stick."*—Take out the key, slip off the cocking collar, unscrew the head of the " stick " by

means of a spanner, and take out the striker, cocking spring and recoil spring.

By unscrewing the nut, the firing collar with lever and safety device can be removed.

13. *Care of the Bomb-Thrower.*—The bright parts must be kept clean and well oiled, and the bomb-thrower thoroughly cleaned after firing, or when it has become wet.

14. *Weights* :—

					lbs.
Bomb-thrower	...	...	...	...	about 31
Bed plate	...	...	...	...	,, 48
Case containing tools and spare parts					,, 24
1915 pattern stick-bomb		...	...		,, 4

15. *Practice Stick-Bombs* are the same shape as the live bombs ; they are painted red.

(b) *The* 1916 *Pattern Bomb-Thrower* (" *Granatwerfer* 16 ") *for Stick-Bomb* (" *Wurfgranate* " 15).

1. *The Bomb-throwers* (Plate XXVI, Fig. 2), consists of the bomb-thrower proper, the traversing arc, and the bed plate.

The bomb-thrower proper consists of the "stick," the body with clamping arrangement, and the sole plate with clinometer and V-shaped back sight.

The bed plate is flanged in front. On the bed plate are two range tables, one for high angle and the other for flat trajectory fire.

The traversing arc revolves on the bed plate and is secured to it by a vertical clamp screw with handle.

With the bomb-thrower is also a box containing tools and spare parts.

2. For description of 1915 pattern stick-bomb and fuze, preparation of bomb for use, and packing of bombs, *see* paras. 2, 3, 4 and 5 on pages 34 and 35.

3. *Installation and Handling of the Bomb-thrower.*—Before use, the smooth working of the bomb-thrower will be tested, especially as regards the firing arrangement, special care being taken that the " stick " is screwed in firmly.

Owing to the recoil, the bomb-thrower is best worked from

the side, preferably from the left, so that the graduations on the clinometer can be read.

The recoil can be checked by a sand bag, which should, however, be placed sufficiently far back to allow of the bomb-thrower sliding freely on the bed plate, so that the position of the latter does not alter. The flange on the bed plate should be well sunk into the ground (handle forwards).

Place the bomb-thrower on the bed plate, taking care that it fits close against the traversing arc.

4. *Laying for Line.*—Revolve the bomb-thrower and traversing arc on the bed plate and sight it by means of the back sight on the soleplate and the red line on the "bridge." Clamp the traversing arc.

5. *Laying for Elevation.*—Grasp the "bridge" and loosen the clamp. Raise or lower the "stick," bringing the setting mark on the body opposite to the graduation on the clinometer, corresponding to the range (*see* Range table on page 39). Tighten the clamp. Hook the lanyard on to the firing lever.

6. *To Cock and Set to Safety.*—Throw the cocking lever sharply against the fore stop. This simultaneously cocks the "stick" and sets it to safety. The letter S (*Sicherung*= safety) is then visible (Fig. 2.)

7. *Loading.*—Place the bomb with its shaft on the "stick." On the word "Ready," remove the safety pin.

8. *Firing.*—Disengage the safety cam on the cocking lever by throwing the lever sharply against the back stop. The side painted red and marked with an F (*Feuer*=fire) is then visible. Take cover.

To Fire.—Release the firing lever by giving the lanyard a smart jerk. This can be carried out from any direction. Upon discharge, the indicator bolt jumps to the right from its recess, thus showing that the bolt has been released.

After firing, push the bomb-thrower, which will have jumped back, hard up against the traversing arc.

9. *Precautions.*—*See* para. 11 on page 35.

10. *To dismount the Bomb-thrower.*—Unscrew the "stick" with the special hooked key and remove the buffer spring from the lower part of the "stick." Using both keys, unscrew the head of the "stick." Remove the striker.

Slacken the retaining screw on the right-hand side of the body, pull out the cocking lever sideways and extract the retaining bolt with its spring. Take out the pin of the indicator bolt and remove the latter with its spring.

Pull back the firing lever and remove the bolt and cocking spring.

To take down the firing device.—Insert the finger in the body of the bomb-thrower and press up the trigger bolt, remove the axis of the trigger bolt, take off the firing lever from the outside and the trigger bolt and trigger bolt spring from the inside. The set screw of the screwed bush of the firing lever should not be touched. This set screw is missing in bomb-throwers Nos. 1—200.

To remove the body from the trunnion bearings.—First remove the clamping screw with handle and then the screw retaining the clamp.

Slacken the retaining screw of the trunnion pin (about 5 mm.), slip the trunnion pin through to one side, elevate the body until it clears the clinometer, and remove it by pulling it upwards.

11. *To Mount the Bomb-thrower.*—Reverse the order of the above operations. Should the firing lever work too easily, slacken the set screw of the screwed bush of the firing lever, and screw the bush further into the body, then tighten the set screw.

When putting in the buffer spring, care must be taken to place the wide end foremost so that the spring sits securely in its recess.

The " stick" must be specially firmly screwed on, to avoid breaking the nose of the cocking lever.

12. *Care of the Bomb-thrower.*—See para. 13 on page 36.

13. *Weights* :—

		lbs.
Bomb-thrower	about	53
Bed plate	,,	35
Box containing tools and spare parts ...	,,	20
1915 pattern stick-bomb	,,	4

RANGE TABLE FOR 1915 OR 1916 PATTERN BOMB-THROWER
WITH 1915 PATTERN STICK-BOMB.

RANGE.		ELEVATION IN DEGREES.	
Metres.	Yards.	High Angle Fire.	Direct Fire.
300	328	45	45
290	317	47	42
280	306	50	38
270	295	53	34
260	284	56	31
250	273	59	29
240	262	62	27
230	251	64	25
220	241	66	24
210	230	68	23
200	219	70	22
190	208	71	21
180	197	72	20
170	186	73	18
160	175	74	16
150	164	75	14
140	153	76	—
130	142	77	—
120	131	78	—
110	120	79	—
100	109	80	—
90	98	81	—
80	87	82	—
70	76	83	—
60	66	84	—
50	55	85	—

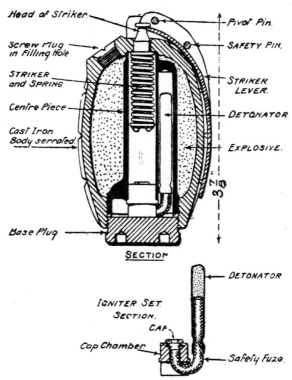

Bomb, Hand, No. 5, Mark I (*Mills Pattern*).
Scale $\frac{3}{4}$.
PLATE I.

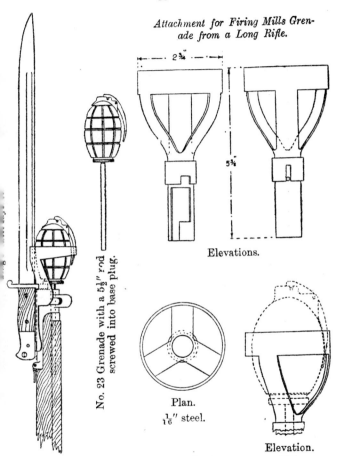

Attachment for Firing Mills Grenade from a Long Rifle.

2¾"

5¾"

Elevations.

No. 23 Grenade with a 5½" rod screwed into base plug.

Plan.
1/16" steel.

Elevation.

Cup Attachment for Firing the Mills Bomb from a Rifle.

PLATE II.

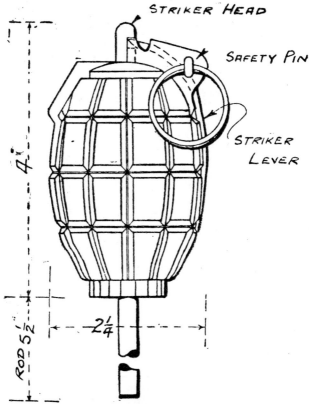

STRIKER HEAD

SAFETY PIN

STRIKER LEVER

4"

ROD 5½'

2¼

Bomb, Hand or Rifle, No. 23, Mark III.
Scale ¾.
See Plate IV for Section.

PLATE III.

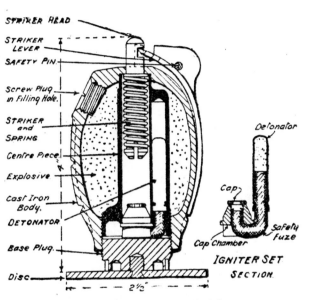

STRIKER HEAD

STRIKER LEVER

SAFETY PIN

Screw Plug in Filling Hole.

STRIKER and SPRING

Centre Piece

Explosive

Cast Iron Body.

DETONATOR

Base Plug.

Disc

Detonator

Cap

Cap Chamber

Safety fuze

IGNITER SET SECTION.

2½"

Rifle Bomb, No. 36, Mark I.

Scale ¾.

PLATE IV.

44

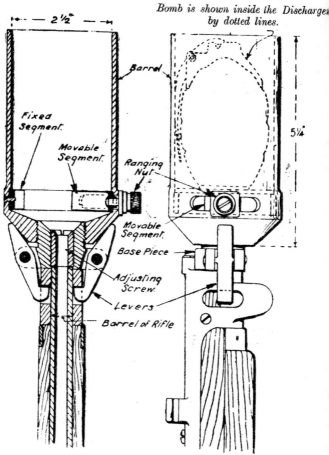

Discharger, Bomb, Rifle No. 1, Mark I.   For attachment to Rifles, short, M.L.E.

PLATE V.

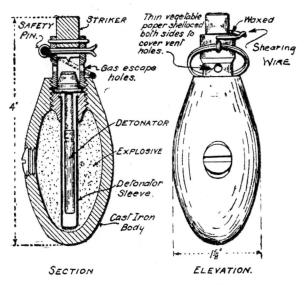

SECTION

ELEVATION.

Hand Bomb, No. 34, Mark III.

Scale ¾.

PLATE VI.

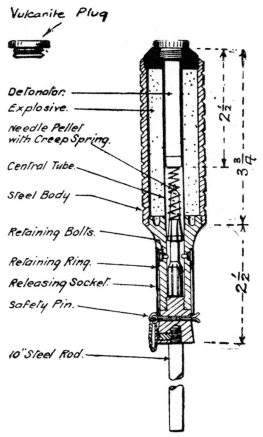

Hales Pattern.
Rifle Bomb, No. 20, Mark II.
Scale ½.
PLATE VII.

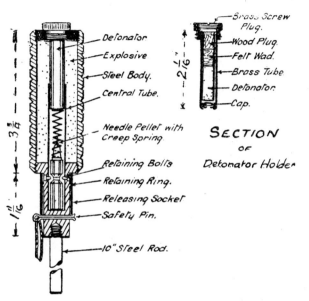

Detonator

Explosive

Steel Body.

Central Tube.

Needle Pellet with
Creep Spring.

Retaining Bolts

Retaining Ring.

Releasing Socket

Safety Pin.

10" Steel Rod.

Brass Screw
Plug.

Wood Plug.

Felt Wad.

Brass Tube.

Detonator.

Cap.

2 4/6"

3 3/4"

1 1/6"

SECTION
OF
Detonator Holder

Rifle Bomb, No. 24, Mark I.

Scale ½.

PLATE VIII.

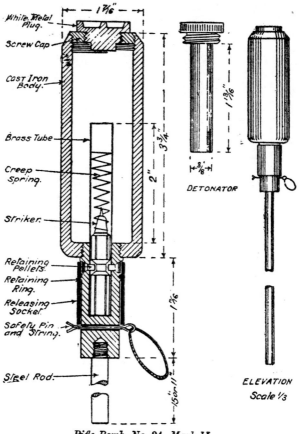

White Metal Plug.

Screw Cap.

Cast Iron Body.

Brass Tube

Creep Spring.

Striker.

Retaining Pellets.

Retaining Ring.

Releasing Socket.

Safety Pin and String.

Steel Rod.

DETONATOR

ELEVATION
Scale ⅓

Rifle Bomb, No. 24, Mark II.
Scale ¾.
PLATE IX.

49

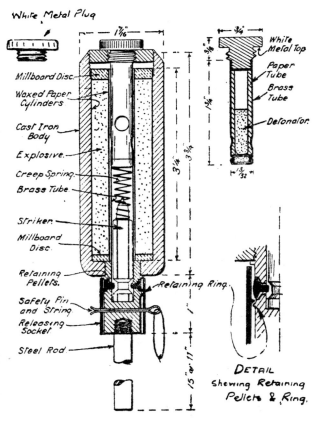

White Metal Plug

Millboard Disc.

Waxed Paper
Cylinders

Cast Iron
Body

Explosive.

Creep Spring.

Brass Tube.

Striker.

Millboard
Disc.

Retaining
Pellets.

Safety Pin
and String.

Releasing
Socket.

Steel Rod.

White
Metal Top

Paper
Tube

Brass
Tube

Detonator.

Retaining Ring.

DETAIL
Shewing Retaining
Pellets & Ring.

Rifle Bomb, No. 35, Mark I.
Scale ¾.
PLATE X.

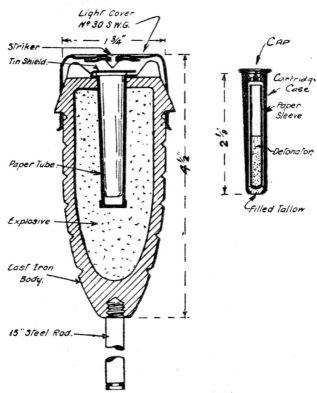

Rifle Bomb. No. 22, Mark 1.
Scale ¾.
Plate XI.

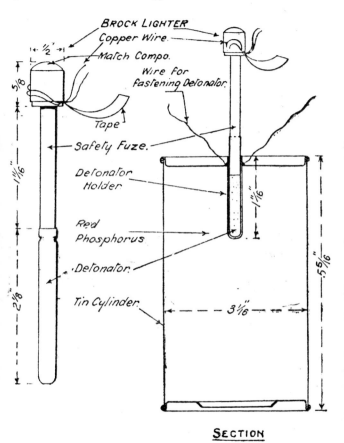

SECTION

"P" Bomb.

Scale ½.

PLATE XII.

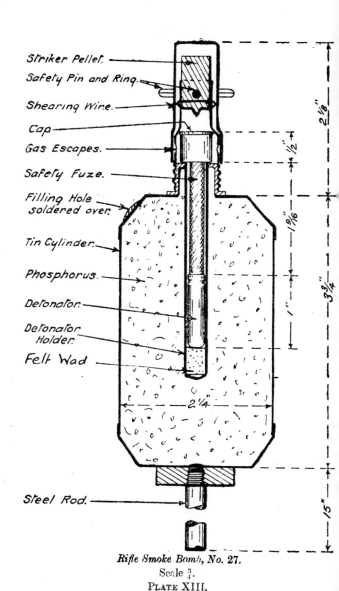

Striker Pellet.

Safety Pin and Ring.

Shearing Wire.

Cap

Gas Escapes.

Safety Fuze.

Filling Hole soldered over.

Tin Cylinder.

Phosphorus.

Detonator.

Detonator Holder.

Felt Wad

Steel Rod.

2⅛″

½″

1 9/16″

1″

3¾″

2¼″

15″

Rifle Smoke Bomb, No. 27.
Scale ¾.
PLATE XIII.

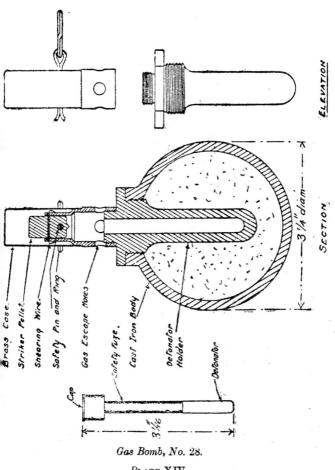

Gas Bomb, No. 28.

PLATE **XIV.**

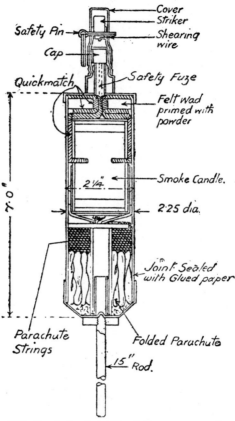

Rifle Bomb, Daylight Signal, No. 31, Mark II.
Scale $\frac{1}{3}$.
PLATE XV.

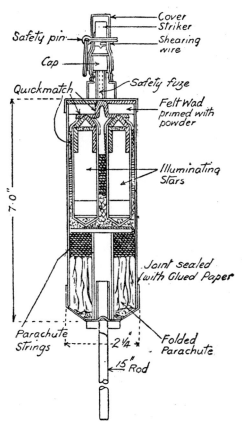

Rifle Bomb, Night Signal, No. 32, Mark II.

Scale $\frac{1}{3}$

PLATE XVI.

FIG. 1.   FIG. 2.

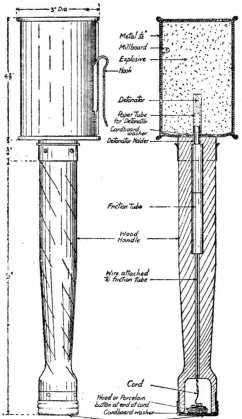

ELEVATION.   SECTION.

Stick Hand Bomb (Time).
(Cylindrical Hand Bomb with Handle.)

PLATE XVII.

PLATE XVIII.

Use of Stick Bomb for firing Bangalore Torpedoes.

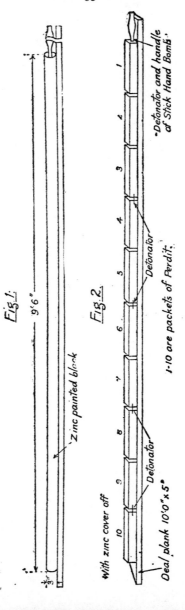

Fig 1.

9'6"

Zinc painted black

3"

Fig 2.

with zinc cover off

1 2 3 4 5 6 7 8 9 10

Detonator and handle of 'Stick Hand Bomb'.

Detonator

1-10 are packets of Perdit.

Detonator

Deal plank 10'0" x 5"

Fig. 3

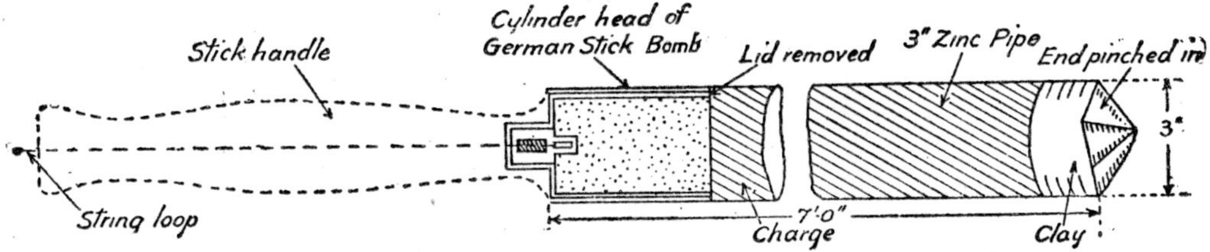
Cylinder head of
German Stick Bomb
Stick handle
Lid removed
3" Zinc Pipe
End pinched in
3"
String loop
7'0"
Charge
Clay

Fig. 4.

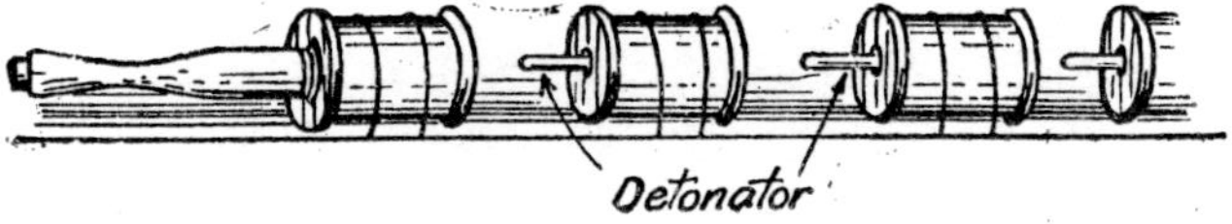
Detonator

Fig. 5.

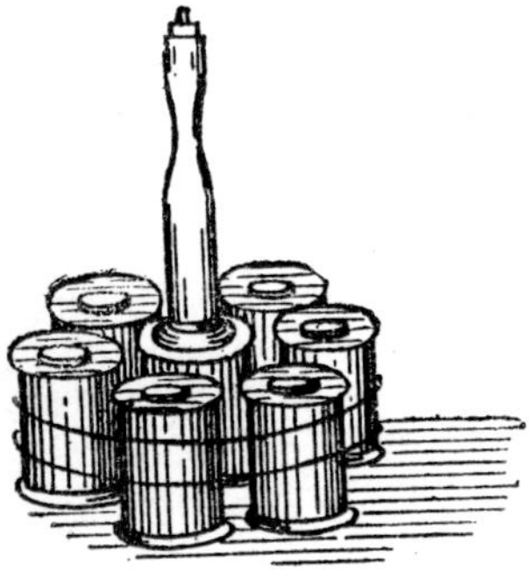

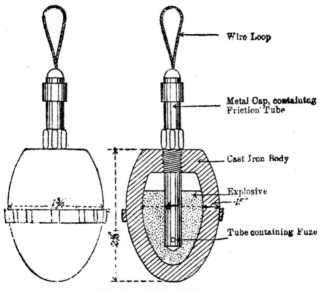

Egg Hand Bomb (Time).

The form of the exterior differs slightly. Some Eggs
have no segmented ring round their middle.

PLATE XIX.

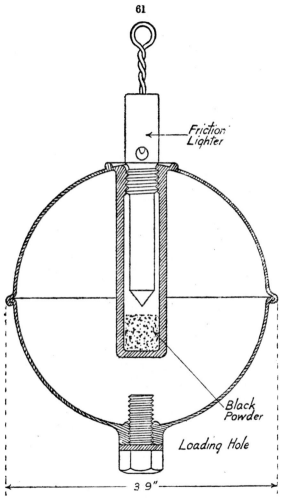

Smoke or Gas Hand Bomb (Time).

PLATE XX

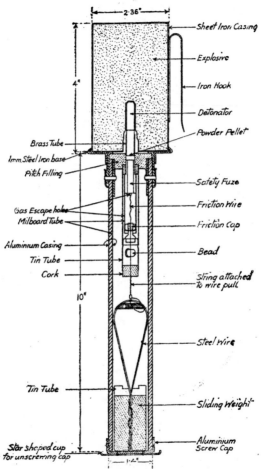

Automatic Lighting " Stick " Hand Bomb.

PLATE XXI.

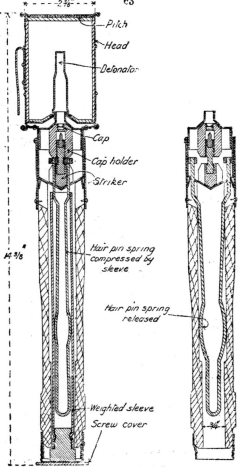

SECTION.

SECTION
SHOWING SLEEVE
WITHDRAWN.

Stick Hand Bomb (Percussion).
PLATE XXII

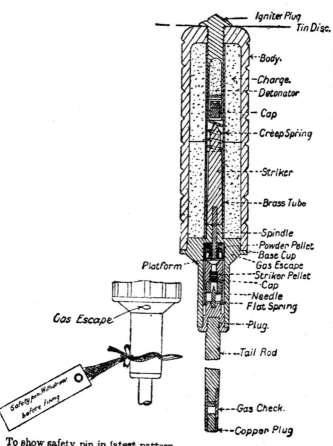

To show safety pin in latest pattern.

Rifle-Bomb, 1913.

PLATE XXIII.

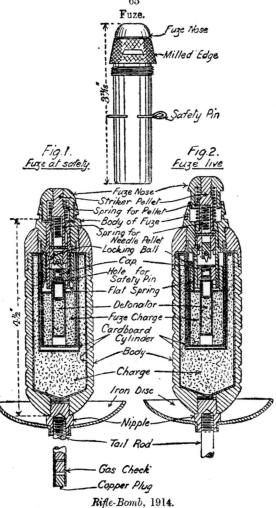

65

Fuze.

Fuze Nose

Milled Edge

3 7/16"

Safety Pin

Fig. 1.
Fuze at safety.

Fig. 2.
Fuze live

Fuze Nose
Striker Pellet
Spring for Pellet
Body of Fuze
Spring for
Needle Pellet
Locking Ball
Cap
Hole for
Safety Pin
Flat Spring
Detonator
Fuze Charge
Cardboard
Cylinder
Body
Charge
Iron Disc
Nipple
Tail Rod
Gas Check
Copper Plug

4 1/2"

Rifle-Bomb, 1914.
PLATE XXIV.

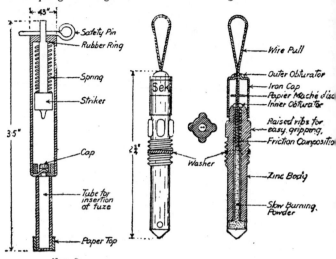

Fig. 1.
Brass Spring Fuze Lighter.

- 43"
- Safety Pin
- Rubber Ring
- Spring
- Striker
- 3·5"
- Cap
- Tube for insertion of fuze
- Paper Top

Fig. 2.
Friction Lighter.

- Wire Pull
- Outer Obturator
- Iron Cap
- Papier Maché disc
- Inner Obturator
- Raised ribs for easy gripping.
- Friction Composition
- Zinc Body
- Slow Burning Powder
- Washer
- 2¾"
- Sek

Fig. 3.
Friction Lighter.

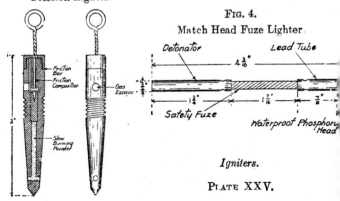

- 3"
- Friction Bar
- Friction Composition
- Slow Burning Powder
- Gas Escape

Fig. 4.
Match Head Fuze Lighter.

- Detonator
- Lead Tube
- 4 3/16"
- Safety Fuze
- 1 3/16"
- 1 7/16"
- 7/8"
- Waterproof Phosphorus Head

Igniters.

Plate XXV.

FIG. 1.—1915 PATTERN.

Cocked, at safety and loaded

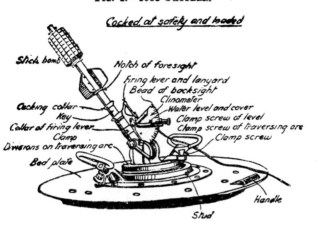

Stick bomb

Notch of foresight
Firing lever and lanyard
Bead of backsight
Clinometer
Water level and cover
Clamp screw of level
Clamp screw of traversing arc
Clamp screw

Cocking collar
Key
Collar of firing lever
Clamp
Divisions on traversing arc
Bed plate

Handle
Stud

FIG. 2.—1916 PATTERN.

Right hand view.

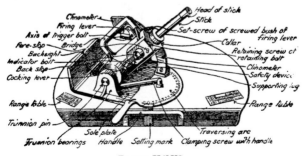

Clinometer
Firing lever
Axis of trigger bolt
Fore-slop
Backsight
Indicator bolt
Back slop
Cocking lever

Head of stick
Stick
Set-screw of screwed bush of firing lever
Collar
Retaining screw of retaining bolt
Clinometer
Safety device
Supporting lug

Range table

Bridge

Range table

Trunnion pin

Trunnion bearings
Sole plate
Handle
Setting mark
Traversing arc
Clamping screw with handle

PLATE XXVI.

68

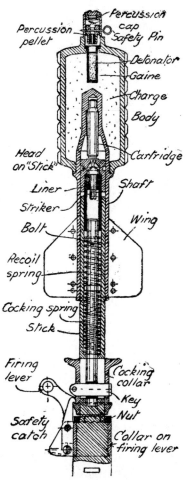

Section through "stick" of bomb-thrower showing bomb in position.

PLATE XXVII.

NSTRUCTIONS ON BOMBING.
PART II

ISSUED BY THE GENERAL STAFF

0/W.O./4483

PART II.
TRAINING AND EMPLOYMENT OF BOMBERS.

November, 1917.

This publication cancels:-
  S.S. 126 "The Training and Employment of Bombers"
    (Revised Edition, September, 1916).
  S.S. 406 "Precautions necessary when Firing Rifle Grenades"
    (April, 1916).
  A.C.I. 289 and 2221 of 1916.
  A.C.I. 214 and 762 of 1917.

(в 13481) Wt. w. 22 8 — P l'336 50 м, 12/17 H & S P. 17/713 (S)

CONTENTS.

CHAPTER I.

PRINCIPLES AND SYSTEM OF TRAINING.

	PAGE NUMBER.
SEC.	
1. General Principles	5
2. Organisation	6

CHAPTER II.

TRAINING.

3. Elementary	7
4. The bombing section	12
5. Method of working down a trench	15
6. Use of rifle and bayonet when attacking round a traverse...	16
7. The rifle-bombing section	19
8. Blocking trenches against a bombing attack	20
9. Collective training	26

CHAPTER III.

SYLLABUS OF TRAINING AND STANDARD TESTS.

10. Recruit training	27
11. Elementary training of sections	27
12. Advanced training	28
13. Syllabus of a 3 days' course	29
14. Standard tests	30

CHAPTER IV.

EMPLOYMENT OF BOMBERS IN THE ATTACK.

15. General principles	33
16. Trench raids and local offensive actions	34
17. " Mopping up "	37
18. Dealing with local opposition during the advance	38
19. Fighting in the open : woods and villages	40

CHAPTER V.

EMPLOYMENT OF BOMBERS IN DEFENCE.

20. General principles	41
21. Counter attack	43

A 2

CHAPTER VI.

CARE AND STORAGE OF BOMBS.

		PAGE NUMBER.
Sec.		
22.	Out of trenches...	44
23.	In the trenches...	45
24.	Other instructions	46

CHAPTER VII.

SUPPLY OF BOMBS.

25.	General principles	47
26.	Supply of bombs in trench warfare, including raids and local offensive actions	48
27.	Supply of bombs in general offensive action, against an organised system of trenches	48
28.	Method of carrying bombs and numbers carried	49

CHAPTER VIII.

DUTIES OF BOMBING OFFICERS.

29.	The battalion bombing officer	53
30.	The brigade bombing officer	54

CHAPTER IX.

PRECAUTIONS AGAINST ACCIDENTS DURING INSTRUCTION.

31.	Precautions at lectures and practice...	55
32.	Method of destroying bombs which have been thrown or fired, and fail to explode	58
	Plates I to XIV.—Methods of Throwing and Firing. ...	61 to 72

CHAPTER I.

PRINCIPLES AND SYSTEM OF TRAINING.

1. *General Principles.*

1. The bomb is a weapon used by the Infantry soldier to supplement his primary weapons, the rifle and the bayonet.

2. The main functions of the bomb are to kill the enemy underground or behind cover, and to force him into the open in order that he may provide a target for the rifle, the Lewis gun, and the machine gun.

A bombing attack unaccompanied by an attack above ground is seldom of any value.

3. Every infantry recruit must receive instruction in bomb throwing, and must know how to use the Mills hand bomb, and have thrown three live ones in practice.

Fifty per cent. of recruits should receive instruction in the use of the rifle-bomb.

4. Men of bombing and rifle-bombing sections, in addition to their normal infantry training, require special instruction in the use of their supplementary weapons, and in working as a team.

5. Cavalry should have sections of bombers and rifle bombers trained for use in the trenches. Each troop should have one section of bombers and one of rifle bombers.

6. All infantry officers should have some knowledge of the technicalities of bombs and rifle bombs. and be thoroughly trained in their tactical use.

7. The responsibility for giving all men a practical knowledge of the use of hand and rifle-bombs rests with company and platoon commanders. One officer per company should be specially trained in bombing work, and one N.C.O. per company should be selected to assist in training and in

supervising the supply and storage of the bombs on charge of the company.

8. Brigade classes to train battalion instructors and expert bombers should be held as laid down in S.S. 152, revised edition, Sec. 5, para. 9.

9. Each battalion should have a specially selected officer, or serjeant, to carry out the duties of battalion bombing officer. Each brigade should have a bombing officer, who is assisted by a serjeant. The duties of battalion and brigade bombing officers are laid down in Chapter VIII.

2. *Organisation.*

1. Every platoon consists of 4 sections, among which are included :—

> 1 section of bombers.
> 1 section of rifle bombers. (See S.S. 143.)

2. Sections must be with their platoons when company training for attack and defence schemes is in progress. For any particular operation, when a special organisation of bombers becomes necessary, a proportion of the bombers of the company may be withdrawn and specially trained under the battalion bombing officer. The normal organisation should be resumed as soon as the operation is over.

Special care must be taken to ensure that men employed as bombers maintain their efficiency in the use of the rifle and bayonet, and in the ordinary duties of the infantry soldier.

3. Bombing sections of one N.C.O. and eight men will normally comprise two bayonet men, two throwers, two carriers (reserve throwers), one rifle bomber, one spare man (sniper or rifle bomber) and the leader (N.C.O.). The section may be divided into two groups, if necessary.

4. Every man of the section should be trained in the duties of each number, so that he can take any place in the section. If this is done the composition of the section can be varied to suit circumstances.

CHAPTER II.

TRAINING.

3. *Elementary.*

1. The object of *elementary* bomb training (which every infantry soldier should receive) is :—

(i) To give the individual a practical knowledge of the bombs in use.
(ii) To teach him how to throw or fire them.
(iii) To make him acquainted with the general principles of the duties of bombers and rifle bombers in trench fighting and in open or semi-open warfare.

A fair standard of accurate throwing with dummies and a working knowledge of the mechanism of the Mills bomb must be acquired before a man is allowed to handle a live one.

The action in throwing is that of overhand bowling. In the case of a right-handed thrower the body is turned half right, the right hand drawn back and below the waist, arm straight. The left arm is carried forward, arm straight. The left foot is advanced, the weight of the body being on the right foot, body bent back, eyes fixed on the mark (see Plate 1). The bomb is hurled with a circular swing of the right arm over the right shoulder, at the same time the weight of the body is thrown forward on to the left foot, every muscle being brought into play. Expert bombers usually impart a pin to the bomb; the bomb should leave the hand at the highest point of the swing and should be thrown well into the air. For short distances it can be lobbed from the shoulder by an action similar to that employed in " putting the weight." A bomb may also have to be thrown with a bent arm from positions in a deep trench where a full swing is not possible, and this should be practised.

Men must be taught to throw or fire from a standing, kneeling, and prone position.

Distance is important in bomb throwing, but accuracy is essential. Bad direction results in waste of bombs and gives confidence to the enemy. Men must be taught to throw at a definite mark at a known distance even in the stages of preliminary throwing practice in the open. They must be taught to keep their eyes on or in the direction of the target while withdrawing the safety pin.

2. Men must be trained so that the removal of the safety pin before throwing or firing becomes instinctive. The withdrawal of the pin and the throwing of the bomb should be regarded as one action. Men should also be practised in withdrawing hooks or keys. Practice " by numbers " is of value in the initial stages of training.

Even when using dummies men must always go through the motion of withdrawing the pin before throwing or firing.

Men should be taught that, if a bomb with a time fuse like the Mills is dropped in the act of throwing, there is ample time to pick it up and throw it out of the trench before it explodes, and that they must do this immediately.

In throwing a percussion bomb from a trench care must be taken not to strike it against the back of the trench, or this may cause it to explode.

3. There should be a prepared training ground at all rest billets, so as to prevent delay in training when battalions come out to rest. (Sec. 152, revised edition, Sec. 7, para. 2)

A good method of preparing the ground is to mark on it a series of double lines, each double line being 3 feet wide, to represent the width of a trench. The base lines, also 3 feet apart, between which the throwers stand, should be 20 yards from the first double line—then four more rows beyond the first one, at distances of 25 yards, 30 yards, 35 yards and 40 yards.

Having once mastered the first distance, the men should then throw at the further distances in turn.

The squads can be divided into two groups of four men, one group returning the dummies to the group throwing from the base line ; by this means no time will be lost and every man will be kept interested in the proceedings.

As soon as the man has attained a certain amount of proficiency in throwing in the open, he should be practised in throwing from behind cover, which is the normal condition under which bombs are thrown in action.

"Cages," as described below, are suitable for throwing practice; they require little material either for construction or upkeep. They are especially suitable in low-lying districts where trenches cannot be kept dry.

All stores of this description should be handed over from one unit to another as billet stores.

4. Instruction should also be given in indirect fire, one man observing, the other throwing. The observer corrects the thrower's aim by calling out after each "dummy" is thrown :—" Shorten six," " Two right," &c.

The following is an example of the method of correction which should always be used by the observer :—

Before a throw—

" 30 front (half right half left) " (to give thrower the distance and direction of the target).

After a throw—

Lengthen 10 (to correct distance).
Shorten 5 (to correct distance).
5 right (left) (to correct direction).
Range (if the bomb has fallen in the right place).

As soon as a good standard of accuracy has been reached, the men should be formed into sections and instructed in trench work. As this instruction is an important part of a bomber's training, it should be progressive and carefully thought out, the practice being conducted at first as a drill in which all detail is explained and all faults corrected. The practice should be gradually quickened up, and the party allowed to work by themselves, the practice being criticised on its conclusion. The importance of each member of a section being conversant with the duties of every number must be remembered, and the numbers changed round accordingly.

5. Cages referred to above can be made as follows (see Fig. 1):

(a) *Throwing cage.*—Consists of 4 posts, which project 8 feet above the thrower's platform. The sides can be made of wire netting or such other material as may be available, and should be blinded, if possible. The front face should be boarded, of which the top 1½ feet can be removed about 6 inches at a time. The thrower stands inside the cage and throws over the front face, the height of which can be adjusted, according to the proficiency of the thrower, either to a height of 6 feet, 5 feet 6 inches, 5 feet or 4 feet 6 inches by removing one or more boards. During wet weather a trench board, upon which the thrower can stand, can be placed inside the cage.

(b) *Target cage.*—The target cages are similar to the thrower's cage, but the front face need not be boarded, nor need the sides be more than 3 feet high. This cage can be made of any length and traverses placed in it at any interval desired. The most elementary cage would be placed in direct prolongation of the thrower's cage; by placing others at different angles the bomber can be practised at throwing at different angles as his proficiency increases. These cages are of particular value in elementary instruction, as the thrower, after completing his practice, can see the result of his throwing.

Throwing Cage.

Plan.

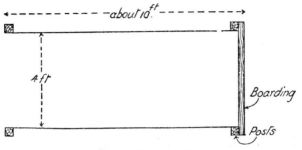

Perspective elevation.

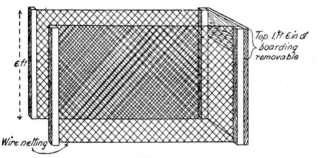

Fig. 1.

6. The following are points requiring attention during training :—

    (*a*) Physical fitness. Bombers should be exercised daily in running, marching, physical drill, &c., to keep them fit and supple.

(b) **Throwing practice should be carried** out daily, but should not be overdone.

(c) Practices in the attack, including an advance over the open, progressing laterally from a section of captured trench by bombing over the traverses, and working down communication trenches.

(d) Defence practice should be carried out. The method of repelling a bomb attack down a trench should be practised, as also the methods of blocking a trench against a bombing attack.

(e) After the initial stages it is essential that men should be trained in throwing under service conditions as regards equipment, steel helmets, carriers, &c. Throwing must be practised when wearing gas helmets or box respirators.

(f) Accuracy of length is just as important as accuracy of direction.

(g) Various types of trenches should be provided to enable practices to be properly carried out, e.g., traversed fire trenches, zig-zag communication trenches with island traverses, &c.

(h) Practice with live bombs at night is necessary.

7. As many men as possible should be instructed in the use of enemy bombs.

4. *Bombing Section.*

The duties of the various men in the bombing section of 1 N.C.O. and 8 men organised for an attack along a trench are as follows :—

Nos. 1 *and* 2, *Bayonet men.*—Their duties in action are to attack the enemy with the bayonet and clear the way for further progress ; and also to protect the men behind them by rifle fire, if necessary.

In trench clearing they will be ahead of the throwers and work round each traverse in turn. It lies principally with the bayonet men to prevent the fighting becoming a mere bomb duel. Once the enemy is on the run, the bayonet men must give him no opportunity to halt and to commence throwing bombs. A rapid and continuous advance is most likely to be successful.

Nos. 3 and 4, Throwers.—These will throw normally under the direction of the section leader. They should watch the movements of their bayonet men, and if the leader is unable to make himself heard, they should regulate their throwing by the position of the bayonet men.

No. 5, N.C.O. or Leader.—He is in charge of the whole section, and is responsible for controlling the fire, preventing indiscriminate throwing, and regulating the advance of the party. He will signal the progress of his party down a trench. Flags, flappers, flares and electric torches may all be used in suitable conditions. In action he will place himself where he can best observe the throwing and control the section. In trench clearing he should usually be behind the first carrier.

He will inspect each man of his party before they start. He will examine the arms of Nos. 1 and 2, and ensure that magazines are charged, that there is one round in the chamber, and that the bayonet is correctly fixed. He will see that Nos. 3 and 4 are correctly equipped, and that Nos. 6, 7, 8 and 9 each have their full equipment of bombs in the carriers, and that each bomb is correctly fuzed. He will make one man of the section responsible for observation to the flanks and for giving immediate warning of counter-attack from the flanks. All the men should know who will take No. 5's place if he becomes a casualty.

Nos. 6 and 7, the Carriers (Reserve Throwers).—They will keep a watch on their respective throwers, and ensure that they always have a bomb handy when required. They must be particularly careful not to follow too closely on their throwers lest they should embarrass them in the act of throwing. They must be ready to replace the throwers in case of casualties.

No. 8, Spare man.—He is second in command of the section and will replace the leader should the latter become a casualty He is, as a rule, responsible for observation to the flanks.

B = bayonet man
T = thrower.
C = carrier.

L = leader (N.C.O.).
S = spare man.
R = rifle bomber.

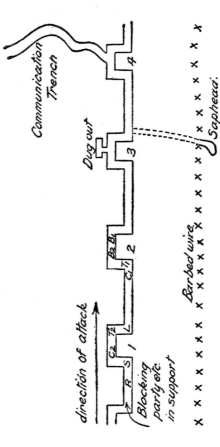

Fig. 2.

No. 9, Rifle bomber.—His duties are to outrange hostile bombers when there is any danger of the attack being checked and thus cover the advance of the section. He can also protect the flanks of the section when required.

Additional rifle bombers or snipers may be included in the section as occasion demands.

5. *Method of working down a trench.*

The following is an example of the method in which a bombing section, organised as in the preceding Section, should be trained to work down a trench (see Fig. 2).

On arriving at traverse 2 the bayonet men should place themselves in positions B1, B2, the first thrower at T1, behind the traverse, the first carrier immediately behind him, at C1. The N.C.O. or leader at L in such position that he can observe the fire and direct his section. The second thrower and carrier will follow next, with the rifle bomber and spare man at the rear of the section.

Crowding must be avoided, and if possible each man should be at a corner, round which he can move to avoid a hostile bomb.

In support, further along the trench will be the blocking parties, riflemen, and Lewis gunners.

As soon as the bayonet men are checked, the leader will direct the first thrower to open fire. No. 1 thrower throws bombs into the section of the trench held by the enemy.

On receiving the word " Report " from the leader, the bayonet men move forward into the next bay and the trench behind the next traverse. If these are clear, " All Clear " is passed back to the leader. The leader then gives the order "Advance," and the whole party advances and takes up positions at traverse 3 similar to those taken up at traverse 2. In this way the party work down the trench.

On reaching a branch or communication trench, or deep dug-out, the leading bayonet man reports to the leader, who decides on the action to be taken.

In the event of a communication trench being encountered, another section would be brought forward to work down it, the first proceeding along the main trench until the objective is reached. If no provision has been made for a second section—the communication trench not being anticipated—the leader should at once send the second bayonet man, thrower and carrier, under command of the spare man, to work a short way down the trench in question.

These will be joined as soon as possible by a blocking party (see Section 8) and riflemen, if considered necessary.

Should an " island traverse " be encountered, the leading bayonet men must watch both sides of it whilst bombs are being thrown.

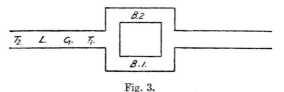

Fig. 3.

In replacing casualties each man should take the place of the man in front omitting No. 5, who is replaced by No. 8.

6. *Use of bayonet and rifle when attacking round a traverse.*

The following is the method of using the rifle and bayonet when attacking round a traverse.

1. *When attacking round a left traverse* (Figs. 4 and 5).

The rifle is held at what may be described as the " low port," *i.e*, slanting across the body, the bayonet pointing upwards and close to the left shoulder ; the left hand close to the left breast and grasping the rifle just behind the piling swivel ; the right hand just behind the backsight.

Left foot forward, and the weight of the body poised for an immediate dash round the traverse with the right foot, at the same time as the bayonet is swung down to deliver a "point."

For an attack round a right traverse—*vice versa.*

Fig. 4.—Attacking round a left traverse. (Back view.)

Fig. 5.—Attacking round a left traverse. (Front view.)

2. *When working round a left traverse to attack an enemy low down on the ground or in a "dug-out"* (Fig. 6):—

Fig. 6.—ATTACKING ROUND A LEFT TRAVERSE, RIFLE HELD
READY TO MAKE A DOWNWARD POINT WITH THE BAYONET.

The rifle point downwards, the small of the butt passing under the right armpit, the point of the bayonet just off the ground ; the right hand grasping the rifle just behind the backsight, left hand just below the piling swivel. The left foot forward and the weight of the body distributed ready to make an immediate dash round the traverse and to deliver a point.

For an attack round a right traverse—*vice versa.*

3. *When moving along trenches in file :*—

The rifle should be carried in the position of immediate readiness, viz., the "low port." In this position the rifles do not protrude beyond the traverse, nor show above the trench.

4. *Instructions to be observed by "bayonet men" :*—

(i) Never go round a corner without being on the alert.

(ii) Learn to use the bayonet with skill when the rifle is gripped behind the backsight with either the left or the right hand.

(iii) Become an adept in all " knock-out " methods with the rifle, and be able to make a " point " even when lying on the ground.

(iv) For night work the bayonet should be dulled.

7. *Rifle-bombing sections.*

Rifle-bombing sections consist of one N.C.O. and eight men. These will normally work in pairs under the section leader, one man of a pair fires while the other observes for him and assists him to load. The loader is on the right of the firer, and he inserts the rifle bomb into the barrel or cup and withdraws the pin. The firer then places a cartridge in the breech and closes the bolt.

(See Plate XIII.)

Sections will be practised in fire control under Section Commanders.

The following descriptions of fire may be employed :—

(*a*) *Individual fire.*—The order " Prepare one bomb— individual fire from the right—. . . . seconds interval " will be given, followed by " No. 1 (right hand man), fire."

The remainder of the section will fire at the given intervals, judging their own time.

(*b*) *Rapid fire.*—The order " Prepare......bombs—rapid fire " will be given, followed by " Rapid fire." On the command " Rapid fire " each man carries on independently until he has fired the number of bombs ordered.

(*c*) *Volley firing.*—The order " Prepare ...... bombs volley fire," will be given, followed by " Section— fire."

Ordinary musketry orders as to range and target will be used.

8. *Blocking trenches against a bombing attack.*

1. Bombers must have a knowledge of the best methods of blocking a trench. In all attacks they should be supported by a party of men, with sandbags and tools, under an experienced N.C.O., so that, whilst the bombers are keeping the enemy at bay a strong barricade can be quickly built.

2. It is advisable to work along the trench for a distance of 50 yards or so further than the point to be barricaded in order to drive the enemy back out of bomb-throwing distance. A second barricade of a temporary nature should be erected at this advanced point, and constant fire kept up by the bombers, while a working party rapidly fills in the trench between the advanced and near barricades, placing wire in it to hinder the enemy from digging it out. It is advisable, as a rule, to attach a small number of Engineers to the party, with a view to blowing down the enemy's trench by explosives. As soon as a clear field of fire has been established from the point to be held the bombers retire from the advanced barricade.

3. In making a permanent barricade provision must be made for dug-outs for the bombing party and riflemen. A bomb store should also be built.

4. It is of advantage to dig a sap leading towards the enemy from each side of the trench which has been blocked somewhat in the form of a " trident." Bombs can thus be thrown into the blocked trench from three points simultaneously. (See Fig. 7.)

5. There are two main types of trench which it may become necessary to block :—

    (*a*) The winding communication trench, down which it is impossible to fire. (Fig. 8, para. 6.)

    (*b*) The straight trench with traverses, along which it is possible to fire when the traverses are destroyed. (Fig. 9 and para. 7.)

6. To block the winding trench effectively, a section of it must be absolutely destroyed. The length filled in should

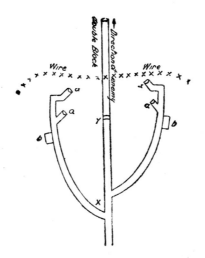

a a a a—Throwing Posts.   *b b*—Bomb Stores.

The point *x* where the foremost sap branches off should be out of bomb-throwing range from *y*, the rear block.

Fig. 7.

be sufficient to give the defence ample time to shoot any men attempting to rush across the gap. An obstacle should be placed across the destroyed portion and continued for 10 yards or so on either side. There is no object in filling in the trench for a greater distance than it is possible to throw a bomb, as it would only be dug out again by the enemy up to the point where our bombs become effective. A barbed-wire knife-rest or similar object placed in the trench before it is filled in will considerably increase the difficulty of any attempt to dig out the destroyed portion.

Should it be possible to fill in only a short length of the

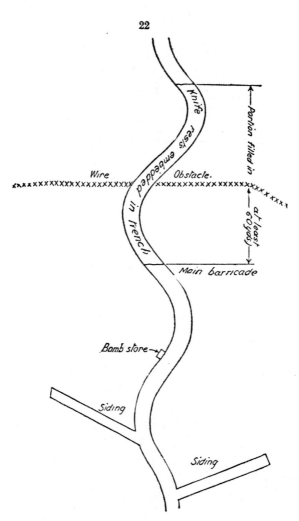

Fig. 8.

trench (15 or 20 yards), the bombers should not be stationed close up to the destroyed portion, where they would be constantly exposed to hostile bombs thrown by men at the enemy's end of the blocked portion. If stationed a little back, they can occasionally run up and throw into the trench beyond the gap. Any attempt on the part of the enemy to dig out their end of the gap should be met by vigorous and continuous bomb throwing until the digging ceases.

In order to guard against a rush across the gap, sidings at right angles to the trench should be made. A Lewis gun is very useful to cover the gap.

These sidings should be constructed as soon as practicable, at intervals in the wake of a bombing attack along a trench :—

(i) To form strong positions on which our bombers can, if necessary, withdraw.

(ii) To relieve congestion of traffic in the trench.

(iii) To provide temporary dumps for reserve supplies of bombs.

7. In the case of a straight trench with traverses (Fig. 9) the traverses in a portion of it should be cut away, and the earth be used to fill the recesses. A strongly built sand-bag breastwork is then made across the trench, with loopholes for observation and fire. The trench behind the breastwork should, when possible, be roofed over to give protection from bombs, with a traverse to protect the men from bombs which burst beyond them. To hinder any attempt of the enemy to rush across the cleared portion of the trench, loose strands of wire should be placed in it. A Lewis gun, if available, can be mounted in the breastwork.

8. In order to guard against damage to the breastwork by bombs continually being thrown and bursting at its foot, a catch-pit can be dug into which bombs will roll before bursting.

Sidings should be made as before.

9. In making a block in a communication trench, care should be taken to level off the earth on either side of any portion of the trench held by us within bomb-throwing dis-

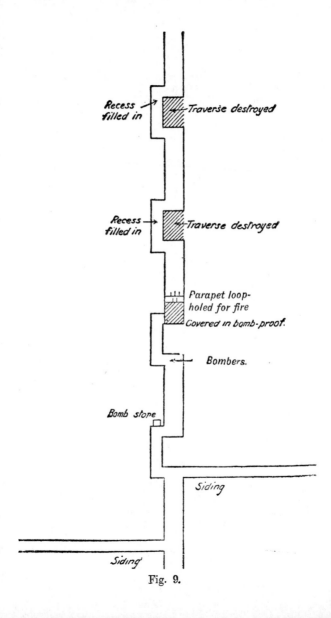

Fig. 9.

tance of the enemy, in order that badly thrown bombs may not roll down the slope into the trench (*see* Figs. 10 and 11).

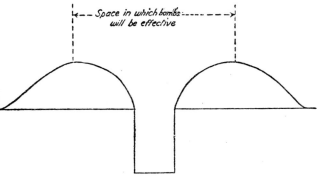

Usual form of communication trench.

Fig. 10.

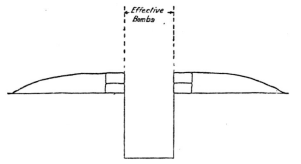

Communication trench with earth levelled off.

Fig. 11.

9. *Collective Training.*

12. Once men are thoroughly trained in the ground work of bombing and rifle-bombing, as much time as possible should be given to tactical schemes. The following points in the course of such training particularly require to be emphasised:—

(i) The bomb and rifle bomb are weapons to be used mainly to kill the enemy underground and to remove him from behind cover in order that he may present a target for riflemen and Lewis gunners.

(ii) The combination of fire and movement, and the necessity for rapid movement, should be explained.

Rapid movement along a trench is difficult. Bombers must learn to work along parapets and parados, and from one shell hole to another, making full use of existing cover.

(iii) In all bombing operations important assistance can be afforded by Lewis guns and light mortars. Such support will only be forthcoming if these arms are kept informed of the actions and intentions of bombing and rifle-bombing sections.

(iv) In addition to being acquainted with the duties of all the numbers of a bombing section, men must be practised in the re-organisation of a section according to tactical requirements, and in the rapid formation of a bombing party in case of emergency, either in attack or defence, from the first men available.

(v) Difficulty is likely to be experienced in keeping the fighting troops provided with sufficient bombs for normal requirements. If indiscriminate throwing or firing be allowed, supplies will fail when most urgently required.

(vi) The use of smoke in the attack, either from 4-inch Stokes mortars, smoke candles or smoke bombs (hand or rifle) should be demonstrated. Smoke can frequently be used effectively by bombing parties in an attack on a hostile machine gun on strong point, or in village fighting, or to screen the retirement of a raiding party.

CHAPTER III.

SYLLABUS OF TRAINING AND STANDARD TESTS.

10. *Recruit training.*

1. All infantry recruits :—

Lectures.—

- (a) General principles of bombing.
- (b) Handling bombs, and precautions necessary in use and storage.
- (c) Description of service bombs (hand) with detailed description of Mills hand and rifle bombs.

Practical.—

- (a) Throwing dummy bombs in open and in trenches, and indirect throwing over screens.
- (b) Throwing live bombs, individual practice.

2. For 50 per cent. of infantry recruits (*see* A.C.I. 1230 of 1917).

Lectures.—

- (a) General principles of rifle bombing.
- (b) Detailed description of service rifle bombs.

Practical.—

- (a) Firing dummy bombs in the open and from cover.
- (b) Firing live bombs, individual practice.

11. *Elementary training of personnel of bombing and rifle bombing sections.*

Lectures.—

- (a) General principles.
- (b) Handling bombs and precautions necessary.
- (c) Description of service hand and rifle bombs.
- (d) Care and storage of bombs.
- (e) Organisation and tactics of bombers and rifle bombers in attack and defence.

Practical.—

    (*a*) Throwing and firing dummy bombs in the open and from cover.

    (*b*) Practices in sections of nine working up trenches with dummy bombs.

    (*c*) Throwing and firing live bombs, individual practice.

    (*d*) Practices in sections of nine with live bombs.*

12. *Advanced training in continuation of section* 11.

The following subjects should be included :—

Lectures.—

    (*a*) Details of bombs and rifle bombs of various types, including the German. (*See* Part I.)

    (*b*) Description of smoke bombs, flares, rockets, &c.

    (*c*) Tactics emphasising the use and limitations of hand and rifle-bombs in attack and defence.

    (*d*) Care, supply and storage of explosives and bombs.

    (*e*) Principles of trench clearing, barricading, and blocking, and consolidation.

Practical.—

    (*a*) Improvement of accuracy and length of throwing hand bombs.

    (*b*) Increased efficiency in use of rifle bombs.

    (*c*) Various practices in attack and defence.

    (*d*) Practice in rapid and continuous throwing.

    (*e*) Throwing and firing at night with live bombs.

    (*f*) Methods of " blocking," barricading and consolidation

Great stress must be laid on throwing discipline. One well-placed bomb is worth any number thrown indiscriminately.

---

* Where conditions are not suitable special dummy bombs may be prepared.

    A type used for practice trench attacks, &c., is made as follows :—

    1. Earth or clay moistened, about the size of a cricket ball.

    2. Empty .303 cartridge case inserted, cap end inside.

    3. The whole roughly stitched up in sandbag material.

    4. Cartridge half filled with black powder, 6 seconds fuze (Bickford) and Nobel Lighter.

This dummy can be used several times by refilling with black powder and inserting fresh fuze and lighter.

13. *Three days' course for bombing and rifle bombing sections.*

Following is a suggested syllabus when only three days are available :—

First day.—Opening lecture on detonators, fuzes, igniters and grenades, and their properties.

Demonstration of action in throwing bombs in various positions in the open by instructor, followed by practice by class. Indirect throwing over screens.

Detailed description of Mills hand and rifle bomb and precautions to be taken with it.

Practice in throwing dummy bombs at various ranges :—

    (i) Into a trench or pit.
    (ii) Out of trench.
    (iii) Over a traverse.

Demonstration of the use of the Mills, Hales and Newton rifle-bombs.

Short drill to demonstrate duties of various numbers in a section.

Second day.—Questions on previous day's work and drill.

Practice in throwing and firing with dummies individually and in groups, in the open and from trenches.

Lecture on care of bombs.

Lecture on organisation and tactics of bombers and rifle-bombers.

Demonstration by trained bombing section of method of working down a trench, supported by a rifle-bombing section.

Third day.—Questions on previous day's work.

Lecture on organisation and tactics of bombers and rifle-bombers.

Individual throwing and hand firing of live bombs.

Practice in sections of nine working down trench with dummy bombs.

Demonstration of method of blocking a trench.

Sections of nine working down trench with live bombs.

14. *Standard Tests.*

1. *First test (with dummies).*—To test accuracy of direction, length of throw, and endurance :—

Position.—Standing in a trench or cage 6 feet wide and throwing over a traverse 6 feet high. The bomber is allowed to jump up to get his direction before throwing, but no mark indicating direction may be used.

Targets (See Fig. 12).—(*a*) Cage (or trench) directly in prolongation of the throwing cage. Height of cage 3 feet,

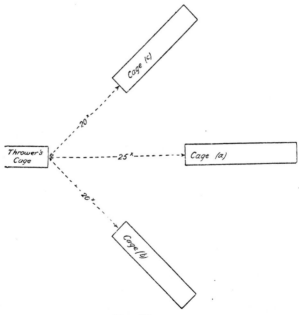

FIG. 12.

width 4 feet, length at least 30 feet. Distance of thrower's traverse to enemy's traverse 25 yards.

(b) and (c). Two cages (or trenches) set at an angle of 45° to the thrower's cage ; same dimensions as for (a), but the distance to the enemy's traverse to be 20 yards.

No. of bombs (dummies), 15.—The bomber starts by throwing into cage (a). As soon as he has thrown three into the cage, he goes on to cage (b) with the balance of the 15 bombs unused ; as soon as he has thrown three into cage (b) he goes on to cage (c) and can expend the balance on getting two into cage (c). If the number of bombs is expended before two bombs have been thrown into cage (c) the bomber fails to qualify. This test is all one test and must be carried through continuously. It must not be divided into three separate tests.

2. *Second test (live bombs).*—Three live bombs to be thrown at a target, the officer conducting the test to decide on the man's capability.

3. *Third test.*—Rifle-bomb. Dummy bomb will be used :—

Target.—A cage (or trench) 20 yards long and 6 feet broad, into which the bombs are to drop.
Distance.—About 70 to 90 yards.
Standard.—Five bombs to be fired, of which three are to pitch inside the target.
Position.—Behind a traverse as in 1. The firer may hold and fire the rifle as desired, so long as his bayonet does not show above the cover.

An observer may be allowed to assist the rifle bomber in this test (*see* Sect. 7).

4. *Fourth test (trench tactics).*—Bombers to be tested by working down a trench or such other exercise as the officer conducting the test considers fit.

Throwers will carry rifles at the short sling on left shoulder, placing these conveniently on ground while throwing and taking up before moving forward

To ensure that each man knows the duties of each number

in a section, numbers should be changed round. Questions can be asked as desired.

5. *Fifth test.*—The officer conducting the test will ask questions to ascertain that the bomber understands the mechanism and objects of all types of bombs in use, including smoke bombs and candles. He should also be asked questions on German bombs.

6. The tests will be carried out in the order named above, except that, if more convenient, test No. 5 may be taken before No. 4.

7. These tests must be strictly carried out and will not be conducted by an officer holding an appointment junior to Brigade Bombing Officer.

The tests laid down in A.C.I. 1230 of 1917 may be carried out by an officer holding a Command or Army Bombing School certificate.

A man must qualify in each test and must not go on to the next until he has qualified in the previous one.

8. *Dress for first, second and third tests.*—Drill order with haversack, waterbottle and entrenching implement, but without rifle for first and second tests.

9. The foregoing tests will be applied at the end of the different stages of training.

(i) All infantry recruits.

Knowledge of Mills bomb.
  (1) How to fuze.
  (2) How to throw.
  (3) Pass Standard Tests 1 and 2 (width of target cage, 8 feet.)

(ii) 50 per cent infantry recruits (see A.C.I. 1230 of 1917).
  (1) How to fuze rifle bomb.
  (2) Pass Standard Test 3 (width of target cage 8 feet).

(iii) Personnel of bombing and rifle-bombing sections.
  Standard Tests 1 to 5.

CHAPTER IV.

EMPLOYMENT OF BOMBERS IN THE ATTACK.

See :—S.S. 143. "Instructions for the Training of Platoons for Offensive Action, 1917 " (O.B. 1919/T).

S.S. 144. "The Normal Formation for the Attack " (O.B. 1914/T), February, 1917.

S.S. 135. "Instructions for the Training of Divisions for Offensive Action " (O.B. 16₅5).

15. *General Principles.*

1. The employment of bombers in the attack may be dealt with under the following headings.

    (*a*) Trench raids and local offensive actions.

    (*b*) General offensive action—

        (i) " Mopping up "—duties in consolidation of positions gained.

        (ii) Dealing with local opposition during the advance.

        (iii) Fighting in the open—attack on strong points held by the enemy, including villages and woods.

2. The organisation of parties will differ according to the requirements of the situation, but the principles remain the same and success will depend on :—

    (*a*) Careful preliminary reconnaissance and preparation.

    (*b*) Every party being given a definite task and organised accordingly ; every man in each party knowing his task and being trained for it ; and sufficient trained men being in reserve to replace casualties.

    (*c*) Accurate and disciplined throwing and rifle-bomb firing.

    (*d*) Arrangements for keeping up a sufficient supply of bombs.

3. In the case of raids bombers will be as lightly equipped as possible. If considered desirable throwers may be allowed to leave their rifles behind. In all other cases the rifle and bayonet will be carried by every number of a bombing section.

16. *Trench raids and local offensive actions.*

1. It will usually be necessary to detail parties of bombers for special duties, such as constructing and maintaining permanent or temporary barricades on the flanks and at previously selected points in communication trenches, clearing portions of the enemy trench system and dealing with deep dug-outs.

2. When preparing for an attack air photographs should be studied so that the best lines of attack may be chosen.

3. All side trenches must be noted and orders given whether they are to be :—

(a) *Picqueted* by bombers and bayonet men as a temporary measure ;

(b) *Permanently blocked,* in which case a working party, as well as the bombers and bayonet men, must be detailed beforehand ;

(c) *Used for a secondary attack,* in which case a properly organised column must be detailed.

A separate party must be detailed beforehand for every side trench. If the air photograph is not sufficiently clear, and side parties cannot be told off for particular trenches, the parties which will be numbered (No. 1 side party, No. 2 side party), will be used as occasion demands.

4. The exact positions for trench blocks will be arranged before the attack, and it is important in order to avoid confusion that the blocks be made actually at these positions.

5. Although special bombing parties may be detailed to clear certain trenches it frequently occurs that the use of the bomb is found to be unnecessary, and that the task can be carried out more rapidly by energetic use of the bayonet. The bomb should not be resorted to unless it is absolutely necessary.

6. Shallow dug-outs should, when possible, be cleared with the bayonet.

In the case of raids, dug-outs should be destroyed, but if a captured position is to be held, the dug-outs will be required by our troops, and should therefore be preserved.

7. Bombers on the flanks of a local attack may at any time be required to work along the fire trench captured with a view to extending laterally the position gained.

8. Rifle-bombers may be used to cover the flanks, to hamper any attempt by the enemy to organise a counter-attack, to engage hostile machine guns within range, and in the case of a raid to cover the withdrawal of our troops.

9. Whenever possible, light mortars should be used to assist bombers. They should be placed to bring concentrated and continuous fire to bear on important points such as trench junctions, suspected machine gun emplacements, &c.

A light mortar detachment working immediately in rear of a bombing section, and shooting 50 or 60 yards in front of the leading bayonet man, can often render useful assistance.

10. Arrangements for the maintenance of adequate supplies of bombs, and for establishing bomb stores in captured positions, must be carefully thought out.

The supply of bombs is dealt with in Chapter VII.

The various accessories required, such as flags or flares to signal progress, electric torches for dug-outs, sandbags, &c., must be provided.

11. The method of attack by a bombing section working down a trench has already been described. (Section 5.)

The necessity for carrying out a bombing attack on a large scale will rarely arise. Experience has shown that a determined, well organised attack over the open is as a rule a more successful and a less costly operation.

12. Should, however, it be decided for any reason to employ bombers on a large scale for operations along a line of trenches in which we have already established ourselves, or to drive the enemy out of a large section of our trenches which he has captured, the attacking party should be organised into :—

    (*a*) Point.

    (*b*) Support.

    (*c*) Side parties (for dealing with side trenches).

    (*d*) Main body.

The composition of these parties will vary according to circumstances. Their duties are as follows :—

(a) *The Point* is the party which makes the actual attack. It will usually consist of one complete bombing section.

The action of the section will be similar to that described in Section 4. Bold rapid movement forward is essential. Volley throwing immediately before each rush should be employed when practicable, throwers distributing the length of trench within range between themselves.

The carriers are responsible for the immediate supply of bombs to the throwers.

Two or three additional rifle bombers working immediately in rear of the Point are valuable.

The duties of the Support, consisting of a complete bombing section are to replace casualties in the Point, to clear dug-outs, and to be prepared in the event of the Point being held up to work round on the flanks, taking what cover they can find in shell holes, &c. The movement of the Support in such case is usually dependent on our own machine guns or Lewis guns and snipers having the upper hand of those of the enemy.

(b) *The Support* also holds any side trench until the arrival of the side party.

The Support is reinforced from the main body and not from the side parties which are immediately in rear of it.

The officer directing the attack should, as a rule, be at the head of the Support. From this position he can combine his duties of regulating the rate of advance and supervising the supplies of bombs, the replacing of casualties in the Point, and the relief of tired men. Relieved men should proceed to a previously selected rallying point, the location of which must be known to all ranks.

An officer or senior N.C.O., according to the importance of the operations, should be detailed to take the place of the officer directing the attack should the latter become a casualty.

(c) *Side parties* form distinctive units and will not be used for reinforcing. The parties will be numbered, each one being detailed to a particular side trench and receiving instructions as to how its trench is to be dealt with and whether it is to be picqueted or permanently blocked. In the latter case a bombing party will be previously detailed from the Main Body.

There should be an officer in charge of the Side Parties.

He will be responsible that each party takes over its allotted side trench, and he will watch for and deal with any attempt by the enemy to counter-attack across the open.

(d) *The Main Body* is responsible for keeping the Support up to its full strength, and will garrison and consolidate all ground won. It is also responsible for organising a chain of supply from the advanced bomb depot to the forward parties.

Some Lewis guns will usually accompany the Main Body. The support of machine guns and light mortars should be arranged, if possible.

17. *Mopping Up.*

1. In the early stages of an advance against an organised system of trenches a certain number of bombing sections will normally be required for special duties both with " mopping-up " parties and with units detailed to garrison captured lines of trenches.

2. Bombers with " moppers-up " will be responsible for :—

(1) Working outwards along the fire trench and establishing connection with units on the flanks.

(2) Picqueting communication trenches.

(3) Picqueting the entrances to deep dug-outs.

On arrival of the garrison the captured line of trenches will be systematically cleared.

Parties of bombers will, as a rule, be detailed to work along communication trenches and to deal with deep dug-outs in the fire trench.

3. Bombing sections will be allotted definite tasks to perform, and their positions in the jumping-off trench will be selected in such a way as to bring them, when they advance, to the point where their duties will begin, *i.e.*, to the entrance of a communication trench to be cleared, or to a previously indicated point in a fire trench where there are deep dug-outs to be dealt with.

Parties will vary in strength and composition according to the length and nature of the trench to be cleared. Usually two or three riflemen detailed to assist each bombing section will be sufficient, but if the trench is a long one and suspected to contain numerous dug-outs it may be advisable to include a Lewis gun section in the party.

The work of trench clearing requires careful organisation to avoid overlapping or the possibility of missing any part of the captured trench system.

4. Smoke bombs are usually effective in clearing dug-outs. If the enemy is in a demoralised condition, hand bombs sometimes serve the purpose, although in a well-constructed dug-out it is probable that the occupants will not be injured.

In cases where the enemy stubbornly refuse to leave the shelter of a dug-out, a light mortar bomb used as a hand bomb is often effective.

18. *Dealing with local opposition during the advance.*

1. Local opposition is likely to be met with at any time in the course of the advance, and unless promptly and boldly dealt with is liable to endanger the progress of our troops on a wide front. Rifle-bombing sections should at once come into action. If not within rifle-bombing range of the enemy they must push rapidly forward under cover of concentrated rifle and Lewis gun fire, until a suitable position is reached. Deliberate rifle-bomb fire should then be opened, under cover of which the remainder of the platoon will advance to the attack.

2. If the wind is favourable smoke rifle bombs may be employed to confuse the enemy and to conceal the movements of our troops.

3. Bombing sections may be required to clear short stretches of trench still held by the enemy.

Fig. 13 shows a likely situation and a suitable formation for a bombing section to adopt.

Rifle-bombing sections should co-operate, keeping up a steady, well-directed fire 30 or 40 yards in front of the bombing section and on any other point that appears to require attention.

The minimum number of men are employed in the trench and the remainder of the section advances on the flanks, moving from one shell hole to another, and throwing into the trench from outside.

This formation, or a similar one, should be adopted whenever possible, for the following reasons :—

(a) Bombers operating over ground get a better view of their target than when working inside the trench.

(b) Maintaining touch with troops on the right and left is facilitated.

(c) The effect of bombs thrown into the trench from either or both sides, as well as from the front, is likely to prove demoralising to the enemy.

(d) Opportunities occur for using rifles as well as bombs.

19. *Fighting in the open—attack on woods and villages.*

1. In open warfare, bombers will not, as a rule, be extensively used. They will, however, probably be required in both village and wood fighting.

2. In house to house fighting, bombers play a prominent part. Bombing parties should be allotted definite tasks in order that the village or town may be systematically cleared. All cellars should be subjected to a thorough search.

Rifle-bombers may be called upon at any period of the operations to deal with enemy machine guns and to remove hostile parties from behind cover. They can provide effective covering fire for troops advancing against enemy positions in enclosed country, in woods and in villages.

3. In the event of troops on either flank of a unit being held up, the commander of that unit, having satisfied himself that his own flanks are secure, will take steps to render what assistance he can.

If the ground forms part of a further trench system it will probably be necessary to employ bombers to extend laterally the ground won thereby approaching the flank of the enemy's

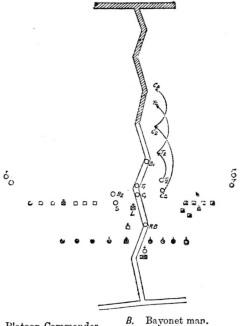

☌ Platoon Commander.	*B.* Bayonet man.
☈ Platoon Sergeant.	*T.* Thrower.
☒ Section Commander.	*C.* Carrier.
☐ Rifleman.	*RB.* Rifle Bomber.
▧ Lewis Gunner.	*L.* Leader (Section Com-
⚲ Lewis gun in action.	mander.
○ Bomber.	*S.* Spare Man (Bayonet Man
⚫ Rifle Bomber.	or Rifle Bomber) to take
⊠ Platoon Headquarters.	the place of the leader
♂ Scout.	if latter becomes a
	casualty.

Shaded trench is held by the enemy.

Fig. 13.—THE FORMATION OF BOMBERS CLEARING A COM-
MUNICATION TRENCH IN AN ATTACK OVER THE OPEN.

Note to Fig. 13.

Men working outside the trench must push forward as rapidly as possible. Their rate of advance should not be regulated by that of the party in the trench.

B2 and S may be on the same side of the trench as T2 and C2, but further to the flank in positions where they can use their rifles to protect T2 and C2 and be ready to replace them.

A method of advance which has proved successful is as follows :—

T2 runs forward, throws into the trench, and at once takes what cover he can.

C2 doubles past him a few yards and does likewise. This is continued until the trench is cleared. (Arrows show their method of advance.)

B2 and S should not as a rule throw, unless the progress of the section is stopped, or T2 and C2 are either put out of action or require relief.

position, and in this way assisting the frontal attack to progress.

Rifle-bombing sections should co-operate in this work.

4. The duties of bombers on reaching their final objective will consist mainly of blocking and barricading, with the assistance of specially detailed working parties, all communication trenches running from the position occupied in the direction of the enemy's lines ; a party of bombers will be detailed to each communication trench.

The bomb should not be regarded as a weapon with which to repel a counter-attack unless such counter-attack is made along a trench.

CHAPTER V.

EMPLOYMENT OF BOMBERS IN THE DEFENCE.

20. *General principles.*

The main infantry defence of a line of trenches will be by rifle, Lewis gun and machine gun fire. Parties of bombers, however, may be distributed throughout the front system of trenches for special purposes. The extent of frontage allotted to a company will be regulated to some extent by the number of bombing sections required for any of the following special duties :—

(a) To hold bombing posts.

(b) To prepare provisional blocks and barricades.

(c) To remain in reserve at selected points for counter-attack along communication trenches in the event of the enemy obtaining a footing in our front line. This will usually be necessary only where the ground is unsuitable for counter-attacking over the open.

2. A " trench " or " bombing pits," dug about 20 yards behind the front trench, from which bombs can be thrown nto the front trench, is an advantage.

Where mine craters, sapheads or hollows exist which neither rifle nor machine gun fire can cover, bombing posts should be established so as to deny such points to the enemy. These posts should be sheltered as far as possible from enemy bombs by wire netting and small traverses.

Saps forward from any trench should be covered to beyond bomb-throwing distance from the trench with a network of overhead wire of about 1 foot mesh. This will prevent parties of the enemy who may capture the sap from throwing their bombs into the trench, but will not prevent the bombs of the defenders from falling among the enemy in the sap. The head of the sap should not be wired, so that when it is occupied by the bombers of the defence they can throw their bombs from it to both front and flanks.

Unless a sap is within bomb-throwing distance of the enemy, occupation by bombers is not necessary; but a bombing post should be established in close proximity to all saps.

The trident trench as a means of defence has already been referred to in Sect. 8 (4). A similar arrangement can be carried out for the defence of a mine crater or at any point where a communication trench joins a main trench, *e.g.*,

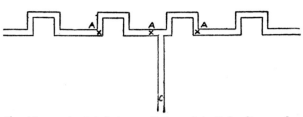

Bombing posts at A.A.A. can all throw into C simultaneously.

Fig. 14.

The action of bombing parties should be laid down in the scheme of defence of each section of the line, and each party should be practised in carrying out its particular rôle, so that every member of it may know what he has to do.

Rifle-bombers should range with "dummies" on our own front line so that in the event of it being occupied by the enemy accurate fire can immediately be brought to bear. Positions from which such registration is carried out and the particular section of the trench to be dealt with from each position require careful consideration.

21. *Counter-attacks.*

1. It is essential that a counter-attack by bombers should start immediately and before the enemy has had time to arrange his defence. In the case of small counter-attacks from the support trenches, the bombing section, which should be permanently stationed close to the communication trench, moves forward at once, followed by the remainder of the platoon. If it is necessary on reaching the fire trench to turn outwards and attack in both directions, two sections should be detailed, one to work to the right and one to the left. Instructions will be issued as to which way the leading section will turn on arrival at the trench junction. If to the right, the left will be treated as a communication trench, and will be guarded by the second bayonet man and second thrower

until the second section comes up; if to the left, the right turning will be similarly guarded.

2. In the case of a counter-attack on a bigger scale from the reserve trenches, a properly organised column with point, support, side parties and main body must be detailed (Section 16, para. 12). The men should be told off beforehand and stationed in the order in which they will advance, *i.e.*, with the point nearest the communication trench. The attack can then be launched at a moment's notice. The men file into the communication trench in order, taking their bombs from the bomb stores as they pass. These bomb stores should be established at the junction of each communication trench with the reserve trench. The bombs should be kept ready packed in carriers.

Such counter-attacks as are described above will rarely take place unaccompanied by counter-attack over the open.

A counter-attack across the open can often be prepared and supported with effect by the fire of rifle bombers.

CHAPTER VI.

CARE AND STORAGE OF BOMBS.

22. *Out of trenches.*

1. Magazine conditions as laid down in Sec. II., paras. 44–46 of Regulations for Magazines and Care of War Matériel should, whenever possible, be observed. These relate to :—

> Prohibition of fires, smoking, &c., in or near such buildings.
> Exclusion from such buildings except on duty.
> Cleanliness and tidiness.
> Doors and windows. Ventilation.
> Examination and unpacking of explosives. Turn-over.
> Moving explosives.
> Punishment for offences.
> Area surrounding magazines.

2. *Sites for stores* should be chosen with a view to :—

  (i) Isolation from areas occupied by troops or civilians.
  (ii) Facility of supply. They should at the same time be suitably distant from roads on which there is much traffic.
  (iii) Natural coolness.

3. *Construction.*—The following points should be considered :—

  (i) Inflammable material should as far as possible be excluded from the building.
  (ii) Stores should be dry both overhead and underfoot. Duck-board floors are often advisable.
  (iii) The stores should be subdivided by sandbag walls into chambers for different kinds of bombs.
  (iv) Ventilation.
  (v) Splinter-proof or, when necessary, shell-proof cover.

4. *Magazine and bomb store regulations*, based on Regulations for Magazines and Care of War Matériel, should be placed in a conspicuous position in all such stores.

Particular regard should be had to the separate storage of all smoke and incendiary bombs. These should be periodically inspected to detect leakage or faulty tins.

Notice boards and danger signs should be conspicuously placed on all approaches.

23. *In the trenches.*

1. *Sites for stores.*—The most important points to be considered are :—

  (i) Facility of supply. Battalion and company stores should be situated near communication trenches. Positions of stores in the fire trenches will be determined by the tactical situation.
  (ii) Normal condition of the ground in the vicinity, and probable results from rain on the positions selected and the approaches to them.

(iii) The possibility of carrying out the work of construction without detection.

2. *Construction.*—

(i) Large stores within the shelled areas are undesirable.

(ii) Splinter-proof and, when possible, shell-proof cover should be provided.

(iii) Ventilation is important. Entrances should be kept open in dry weather and closed in wet.

(iv) Drainage in the vicinity of the stores must be provided.

24. *Other Instructions.*

Instructions as to the following should be issued with regard to bomb stores :—

(i) They will not be used for any other purpose.

(ii) Smoking and the use of naked lights in the vicinity of bomb stores are prohibited.

(iii) No inflammable material is allowed in a store.

(iv) Stores will be clearly marked and, when necessary, approaches to be used by carrying parties will be indicated.

(v) All bombs should usually be fused before leaving Brigade Bomb Stores. They should seldom be taken unfuzed beyond the Battalion Bomb Store. Boxes containing fuzed bombs shall be marked on the lid with white diagonals.

(vi) All bombs sent to the trenches must be constantly turned over. This can be done, if ordinary expenditure is not sufficient, by bringing back bombs* from the trenches and replacing by fresh issue.

(vii) The insertion of detonators should be carried out under the driest possible conditions. The base plug of the Mills bomb should be well smeared with vaseline before it is screwed home.

---

* *Note.*—These bombs may after careful examination be used by instructional classes.

(viii) A supply of vaseline or mineral jelly should be
kept at Brigade and Battalion Bomb Stores and
the bombs should be frequently examined and
kept free from rust, special attention being paid
to the lever and safety pin.

(ix) Careful attention should be paid to the regulation
of ventilation. Entrances should be kept open
in dry weather and covered over in wet.

CHAPTER VII.—SUPPLY OF BOMBS.

(*See* Section XXIV. ss., 135.)

25. *General Principles.*

The general principles of supply are the same in both
defensive and offensive operations, although the application
of these principles will vary.

These principles are :—

(1) A recognised chain of responsibility for supply.
Os.C. companies should be responsible for organising the
supply of bombs to the fighting troops from trench bomb
stores in the case of stationary warfare and from advanced
stores established in captured positions during offensive
operations. These stores are replenished by carrying parties
working under the battalion bombing officer from the
battalion store to the advanced stores, and under the brigade
bombing officer from the brigade to battalion store. The
brigade store is replenished from the divisional ammunition
column.

(2) Preparation of each bomb before it leaves brigade
headquarters by inserting the detonator, and by examining
safety pins to see that they can easily be withdrawn.

(3) A system of supervision of storage of bombs in the
line to ensure that reasonably accurate estimates may be
made of the supplies available or likely to be required.

(4) The number of bombs stored should not exceed
requirements, otherwise the danger of deterioration is in-
curred and unnecessary work is thrown on carrying parties.

(5) An initial supply in bombing posts, &c., in defence, or carried by the men in offensive operations.

(6) Transit of bombs from store to maintain this initial supply.

(7) The arrangements for supply should be made known to all concerned.

26. *Supply of bombs in trench warfare, including raids and local offensive operations.*

(1) It is sometimes possible to employ horse transport or light railways to carry supplies of bombs forward by night from brigade stores to intermediate dumps. These dumps will as a rule be by the roadside or at the head of a light railway.

2. Arrangements should be made for carrying parties to be ready to move the bombs to their proper stores immediately they arrive at these dumps.

(3) In arranging for carrying parties the following points should be observed :—

(i) They must have written instructions as to where they are to go and to whom they are to report on arrival.

(ii) In the case of a raid or local attack, in which a constant flow of bombs to the scene of operations may be necessary, small parties of men carrying for short distances and making a number of journeys over the same ground, are usually more satisfactory than large bodies of men carrying from the source of supply to the fighting troops.

(iii) Near the actual scene of hostilities, where coming and going traffic is difficult, a chain of men passing up bombs is usually a satisfactory method.

27. *Supply of bombs in a general offensive action against an organised system of trenches.*

Prior to the commencement of the advance the following arrangements for supply will normally be made :—

(1) A number of bomb stores will be constructed as near to the jumping off trench as practicable.

The bombs for these stores should be taken forward as soon as possible to stores established in the captured positions.

Battalion and brigade bomb stores will be constructed as far forward as possible. In selecting the positions for these attention must be given to facility of supply, nature of approaches and probable zones of the hostile barrage.

(2) Horse transport or pack animals may be detailed to move forward at certain stages of the operations to selected points. Fuzed bombs should not be carried on wheeled transport if avoidable.

(3) Routes for carrying parties should be carefully reconnoitred so that every advantage may be taken of cover from view and from machine gun and rifle fire, afforded by the contours of the ground, &c.

(4) All bodies of men sent forward in support of the attack should carry bombs. The issue of these bombs should be made from the rearmost stores, if possible, so as not to deplete those further forward. These bombs should be collected and dumped at selected points in the captured positions.

28. *Methods of carrying bombs and numbers carried.*

1. The following patterns of bomb carriers have been found useful :—

(a) *Bucket carrier* (Fig. 15).—This is a canvas bucket with double bottom. It is carried by a sling of adjustable length, and will hold up to 20 Mills bombs. It is closed by a cord.

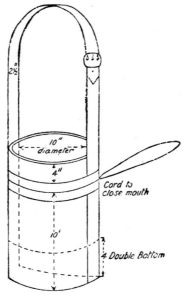

Fig. 15

Care should be taken that the safety pins are not bent when bombs are carried in a bucket

(b) *Belt bag carrier.*—A canvas bag with steel hook, to be carried on waistbelt and holding four Mills bombs.

The bag is closed by a piece of string.

Various other types are in use.

(c) *Waistcoat pattern*, with pockets, to carry 10 Mills bombs.

(d) *Yukon Pack* (Figs. 16 and 17).—Complete boxes of Mills bombs can be carried (see para. 3 (d) (i) below), and this pack is especially suitable in stationary trench warfare.

Fig. 16.—CARRYING BOXES OF MILLS BOMBS IN A YUKON PACK (BACK VIEW).

In offensive operations it will be used as far forward as practicable, but bombs must be removed from their boxes, and transferred to bucket or other carriers before being

handed to the troops actually in touch with the enemy.
Carrying parties employed so far forward as to be likely to
become involved in the fighting should not be provided with

Fig. 17.— CARRYING BOXES OF MILLS BOMBS IN A
YUKON PACK (SIDE VIEW).

Yukon packs, as their use prevents a man from being fully
equipped in fighting order.
  2. The number of bombs which can be carried by each

man will be determined by the distance he has to travel, the condition of the ground, and the general physique of the man.

These points demand most careful consideration as the overloading of men has frequently had disastrous results.

3. The following approximate numbers are given as a guide :

(*a*) Bombing section.

(i) Bayonet men, throwers, leaders and spare man (if not employed as a rifle-bomber) each man	7 hand bombs.
(ii) Carriers, each man up to ...	14 hand or rifle-bombs.
(iii) Rifle-bomber	7 rifle-bombs.
(*b*) Rifle-bombing section, each man	7 rifle-bombs.
(*c*) All other men taking part in an attack, each man	2 hand or rifle-bombs.

(*d*) Carrying parties.

(i) On Yukon pack (in boxes) ...	3 or 4 boxes, *i.e.*, **36** or 48 bombs.
(ii) Bucket carrier or other means	12 to 14 bombs.

4. The exact proportion of hand bombs to rifle-bombs to be taken forward by men other than those of bombing and rifle-bombing sections will be determined by the nature of the fighting which is likely to take place on the front of the unit concerned.

CHAPTER VIII.

DUTIES OF BOMBING OFFICERS.

(*Vide* Section 2, para. 4, and Section 25, para. 1).

29. *The Battalion Bombing Officer.*

The position of the battalion bombing officer is that of an expert adviser to the battalion and company commanders. The bombers of a battalion are not under his command.

His duties are :—

    (a) In Action.

        (1) To take charge of the battalion bomb store and carriers.

        (2) To keep a record of all supplies of bombs.

        (3) Periodically to visit bombing posts and bomb stores in the trenches.

    (b) In Rest.

        (1) To advise and assist generally in the training of bombers and rifle bombers.

        (2) To arrange for an adequate supply of " dummies " for practice.

        (3) To arrange competitions.

30. *The Brigade Bombing Officer.*

His duties are :—

    (a) In Action.

        (1) To take charge of the brigade bomb store and carriers.

        (2) To keep a record of all supplies of bombs, keep in touch with the Divisional Ammunition Column, and indent on them through the proper channels for bombs required.

        (3) To send up bombs indented for by battalions.

        (4) To visit battalions, and to ascertain their requirements.

        (5) To keep the Brigade Trench Map up to date in all features associated with bombing.

    (b) In Rest.

        (1) To arrange instructional classes.

        (2) To assist and advise battalion bombing officers.

        (3) To arrange competitions.

        (4) To be responsible for carrying out Standard Tests (see Section 14, para. 7).

CHAPTER IX.

PRECAUTIONS AGAINST ACCIDENTS DURING INSTRUCTION.

31. Precautions at lectures and practice.

(1) Live detonators and filled bombs (*i.e.*, bombs charged with explosive) will not be used unless a qualified officer is in charge. The use of all improvised bombs of a dangerous nature, and the carrying out of unauthorised experiments with bombs is forbidden.

(2) Demonstrations with filled bombs will not take place inside any buildings.

(3) Dummy bombs only (*i.e.*, bombs without an explosive charge in them), and dummy detonators only (*i.e.*, models of wood or metal to represent detonators), will be used during lectures.

(4) Dummy bombs and dummy detonators will be specially marked.

(5) A dummy bomb will not be reloaded to serve as a filled one.

(6) Before beginning a lecture or practice in which dummy bombs are to be thrown, the instructor will examine the material very carefully in order to ensure that there are no detonators or filled bombs included in it.

(7) All ranks will be warned that live detonators, filled bombs, and especially filled bombs with live detonators in them (known as fuzed bombs), must be handled with care.

(8) Detonators must never be handled roughly, nor must they be forced into a bomb or holder. If the detonator does not fit easily, another must be used ; the first may possibly be of the wrong type. The discarded detonator must be placed on one side for inspection by the instructor; Detonators must never be left lying about.

(9) Detonators crimped on to safety fuze must never be pulled off ; if it is necessary to remove the detonator, the fuze must be cut above the crimping.

(10) At instruction a reliable man should be placed in charge of the detonators and kept apart from the rest of the party ; he should issue detonators only on the order of an officer.

(11) At practice in inserting live detonators, only one detonator should be used at a time for each party and the men should come up singly, the others keeping at a safe distance or behind a traverse.

(12) The fuzing of bombs by the insertion of the detonator (detonator holder) or igniter will not be carried out in immediate proximity to a stack of bombs or boxes of bombs. There should be a definite place chosen, and a suitable sandbag structure erected consisting of one enclosed compartment for carrying out the fuzing and another into which a bomb can be thrown in the event of ignition taking place.

(13) At all practices with fuzed bombs the instructors and the classes will wear steel helmets.

(14) When under instruction from properly prepared throwing bays, men are not to pick up and throw out of the bay a live bomb which has been dropped. They will at once move into the next bay and leave the bomb on the ground.

(15) During individual practice with fuzed bombs not more than one instructor and the thrower (firer in the case of rifle-bombs), or in all two persons, will be allowed in the throwing trench or pit at the same time ; the remainder of the class will take cover before the bomb is thrown. At least one instructor will be present with these men to ensure that they do not expose themselves.*

---

* The following is a safety arrangement which has been found satisfactory for preliminary instruction in hand bomb throwing :—Bombs are thrown from A. The Instructor's positions until the pupil is actually ready to throw is at C, where he has only a low wall between himself and the thrower. As the pupil throws, the instructor steps forward to B, where he has the high wall between himself and his pupil. A trench can be dug or barricade erected, D, at a convenient distance behind for the accommodation of the remainder of those under instruction, who will come up in turn to throw. Two or more throwing pits can be made according to the

(16). In collective practices, where a section is working down a trench only one man at a time will be allowed to throw live bombs. When rifle-bombs are being fired simultaneously not more than one instructor and the firers will be allowed in the trench at the same time. They should be separated from one another by traverses, the remainder being under cover. Volley throwing with live bombs will not be practised. Though in action it is necessary to throw bomb volleys, in practice the risk outweighs the benefit.

(17) Preliminary instruction of rifle-bombers should include the firing of dummy rifle-bombs, to accustom the men to the position illustrated in Plates VII to XIV.

When live rifle-bombs are used in elementary instruction they should be fired by a lanyard through a box loophole or pipe built in a breastwork or parapet, the rifle-bombs being inserted from the front after the rifle is in position, and not fired until the instructor and the firer are behind the breastwork or parapet. Live rifle-bombs should only be fired in the manner illustrated in the plates, when the men are accustomed

---

number of the class. A supervision post for the officer in charge of the practice can, if desired, be erected in rear of the pit or pits. Its exact position will be selected with a view to facility of control.

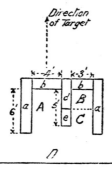

to these positions and are thoroughly acquainted with the rifle-bomb.

(18) During practice with live bombs the danger area must be considered as a circle with a radius of 200 yards from a point where the bomb explodes; no one should be allowed within the danger area except under suitable cover.

(19) In throwing practices from an instructional bombing pit if a live time fuze-bomb fails to explode it should, if possible, be recovered before the practice is continued. It should not, however, be touched before one minute has elapsed, and then only by a qualified instructor, the class remaining under cover.

(20) At the conclusion of any practice with live hand or rifle bombs, the ground should be carefully cleared of all bombs which have failed to explode.

On no account should filled bombs be left lying about.

(21) Should a fuzed bomb not be used, the detonator, or igniter in case of the Mills bomb, will be removed from it as soon as possible, and in any case before it is returned to store; on no account will such an operation be carried out in any bomb store. It must be done on the ground under proper precautions for safety.

(22) The safety fuze in the igniters in Mills hand and rifle-bombs will be examined to see that it is not cracked at the bend as this may cause erratic burning.

(23) The rod of a rifle-bomb should be cleaned and not oiled as the presence of oil may cause a dangerous pressure in the barrel of the rifle.

(24) The special precautions given in the descriptions of the different types of bombs will invariably be observed. (See Part I.).

(25) Inspections should be carried out in a good light.

32. *Method of destroying bombs which have been thrown or fired, and fail to explode.*

1. Fuzed percussion bombs or time bombs, other than Marks No. 5, No. 23 Mark 1 and No. 23 Mark II, which fail to explode, will be destroyed *in situ* without handling.

When a live Mills bomb No. 5, No. 23 Mark I or No. 23 Mark II, fails to explode, at least one minute should be allowed to elapse from the time of failure before being collected.

2. The following stores are required :—

> Guncotton primers 2 oz.
> Rectifiers gun cotton primers No. 5
> Detonators No. 8
> Safety fuze (6 ft. lengths)
> Matches (as required)

Instructions.

3. (a) Take the guncotton primer from its cylinder, remove the waterproof paper holder, and insert the rectifier into the hole in the primer to the full extent to which the detonator is to enter, and withdraw it with a twisting motion. This ensures easy insertion of the detonator.

(b) From each end of the safety fuze remove about one inch of the covering tape, cut the gutta-percha covering with an oblique cut at the end to be lighted, and a clean straight cut at the other end which will be inserted into the detonator.

(c) Fix the detonator with safety fuze attached into the hole in the guncotton primer, and place the whole on the bomb to be destroyed (laying the free end of the safety fuze clear) and cover with six inches of earth, being careful not to disturb the gun cotton primer.

(d) Ignite the free end of the safety fuze, and take cover. The safety fuze burns for about two minutes.

4. If no cover is available no person should be allowed within a radius of 200 yards of the bomb being destroyed.

Special precautions to be observed.

Care should be taken when using the rectifier that no undue friction is caused ; otherwise the guncotton primers may become dangerous through overheating.

Detonators should be handled with the greatest care, as they are highly dangerous in unskilled hands.

On no account should an attempt be made to remove the fulminate of mercury from the detonator for any purpose whatever.

Before they are inserted into a guncotton primer care is to be taken to see that the hole for their reception is large enough for their easy insertion.

On no account is any attempt to be made to force them into position, and screwing or twisting them is to be particularly avoided.

Note.—Plates demonstrating throwing positions should be taken as a general guide, but in the course of training men should be allowed to throw from the position in which it is found the individual obtains the best results.

PLATE I.

Throwing standing from behind Cover.

PLATE II.

Throwing from a Deep Trench.

PLATE III.

After throwing from a Deep Trench.

PLATE IV.

Throwing Kneeling.
Throwing position.

PLATE **V.**

Throwing Kneeling.
Completion of throw and action of falling forward to resume
prone position.

PLATE VI.

Throwing Kneeling
(alternative position).

PLATE VII.

Firing Mills Rifle Bomb (with rod)·
Standing position.

PLATE VIII.

Firing Mills Rifle Bomb (with rod).
Standing position.

PLATE IX.

Firing Mills Rifle Bomb (with rod).
Kneeling position.

PLATE X.

Firing Mills Rifle Bomb (with rod).
Firing from the shoulder.

PLATE XI.

Firing Mills Rifle Bomb (from Discharger Cup).
Removing Safety Pin.
This method is necessary only when rifle bombers are not working
in pairs.

PLATE XII.

Firing Mills Rifle Bomb (from Discharger Cup).

The rifle is held magazine upwards to bring the shock of discharge, which is considerable, on to the heel of the butt, thus reducing the leverage tending to break the stock bolt.

Plate XIII.

Firing Hales Rifle Bomb.
Preparing to fire (prone position).

Plate XIV.

Firing Hales Rifle Bomb.
Ready to fire (prone position).

FireStep
Publishing

FireStep Publishing is a new division of *Tommies Guides Military Booksellers and Publishers*, first established in 2005 by Ryan Gearing. Our aim is to publish up to 100 books and related product a year and bring new and old titles alive for the military enthusiast whilst having the ability and desire through many of our book projects to work with and to suport HM Forces and related charities.

We offer an unparalleled range of services from traditional publishing through to subsidised self-publishing and bespoke packages for the discerning and specialist author, historian, genealogist, museum or organisation. We are always looking for new ideas and ventures and especially welcome enquiries from military museums and organisations with a view to partnering in publishing projects.

We pride ourselves on our commitment to each book and our authors, our professionalism and being able to work solely within the military genre, with the knowledge, contacts and expertise to maximise the potential of any of our products.

For more information on any of our titles, to contact us with suggestions for new books, or just to keep in touch please visit our website: www.firesteppublishing.com